Judas's Mother

A Parable Freeing Maternal Guilt

Judas's Mother

A Story for Every Mother Who Feels Responsible
For the Choices of Her Children

Bobbi Sims

To Nan –
Be Blessed,
Bobbi Sims

Élan Publishing
Texas

Library of Congress Cataloging in Publication Data

Sims, Bobbi

ISBN 1-879521-36-9

Printed in the USA

First Printing September, 2004

Book design by Laurie Burke

Cover design by Samantha Wall

Élan Publishing

4600 Ocean Drive Suite 408

Corpus Christi, TX 78412

Web site: http://www.JudasMother.com

In Memory of
David

Dedicated to
Adele Farrell, for her encouragement to me
to write this story;

to every mother who has experienced the
depth of pain through losing a child;

to every mother who has suffered guilt, shame,
and inordinate responsibility for the choices
of her children;

and to every mother who desires to rear her
children to be responsible adults.

Chapter 1

I awoke early, before the servants. The excitement of last night's Passover feast escaped me this morning. Concerned over rumored plots by the Pharisees against the life of Jesus, my husband Simon abruptly left for the Temple the minute the celebration ended. Neither Simon nor Judas returned home last night. My heart raced with fear. *Where in the world could they be?*

To avoid apprehension, I busied myself with needlework. Eager to try new bone needles purchased from a street vender, I started work on embellishing a girdle for Judas. The fine needles easily worked the fabric. The intricate embroidery lessened my anxiety as I anticipated Judas's delight when I presented it to him.

Startled, I looked up, greatly relieved to see Judas. Somehow, he appeared much taller than his actual height with thick, dark curly hair and beard completely disheveled. Just having him home gave me comfort and I immediately anticipated the news about where Jesus would be teaching, but then I saw his eyes—eyes glistening with inexpressible sorrow.

As he drew near, his deep voice trembled, "I am the one."

"What do you mean, Judas?"

"I am the one who did it."

"Did what?" I shouted, my heart pounding with fear.

"I'm the one who surrendered Jesus to the Pharisees."

My heart seemed to leap into my throat, choking me. Unbidden tears blurred my sight as I sought the meaning of Judas's words.

"No, you didn't!"

"Yes! I turned him over to the priests."

"Judas! Why are you saying this? I've been sleepless and worried without word from you or from your father. I don't want to hear this! This must be too much wine talking. I will hear no more lies."

My hand flashed out. I can still hear the sound it made as it struck his face.

He looked stunned, but mumbled, "Yes, I did."

Clasping my hands over my ears, I closed my eyes tightly to shut out his tortured features. My body flinched as he tried to grasp my hand. I spun away and stumbled toward the wall. I could not bear to hear the words Judas kept repeating. Gasping, I stared at him in disbelief. His eyes rested upon my horror-stricken face and stiffened body. After gazing at me in agony and longing, he turned away. Without another word, he left the house. From my window, I could see him on the walk outside the house. Turning slowly, Judas took one last look at the home where he had grown up and the garden he loved so well; then listlessly, he walked away.

My heart pounded. In my confusion and desperation, I tore at my hair and cried out. I slowly wandered through the house, into the garden and sank onto the nearest bench. I sat staring at nothing in stunned silence. My mind searched for some semblance of reason for Judas's incomprehensible behavior. Finally, I convinced myself this horrible encounter held no truth. Surely, he was drunk.

Even so, I still tried to make sense of my son's declaration. I thought, *"He simply must have suffered too much strain and worry about Jesus' safety. His devotion to Jesus caused him to fear betrayal and the new wine tricked him into thinking he did the deed Jesus had spoken of earlier in the upper room."*

Fear crept deeper into my mind. Last night Jesus did say someone would betray him. For a moment, I considered Judas knew something of what he said. I dismissed the possibility immediately.

My thoughts darted like frightened birds seeking a safe haven. I sat in the no longer peaceful garden, and pondered, *"Who among the twelve could really be the betrayer?"* Each one of them voiced self-doubt.

"It cannot be Judas!" I whispered aloud to the silent garden; yet Jesus' words from the night before rang in my ears— *"but one of you is consumed by a burning obsession."* Even I used those words to describe my son on many occasions. Had Judas's passion been misled?

My restless gaze fell upon the now useless sewing lying crumpled in the doorway. Slowly, I rose, gathered the fabric to my breast, and drifted into the house. The fabric fell from my fingers onto the nearest chest. Staring at it, I vowed never to touch it again. I sat in numbed silence for what seemed like hours.

With relief, I heard my dearest friend, Amashia, calling my name as she neared the door.

"Amashia, I'm so glad to see you! Judas came home this morning. He told me he turned Jesus over to the Pharisees. Of course, I did not believe him. I do not know why he would say such a thing unless he drank too much wine. The worry and concern he has for our Master has left him confused. It just couldn't be!"

Full of distress and heavy sorrow, I tried to convince Amashia and myself of the truth of my words

Amashia put her hand on my shoulder to console me. "My precious friend Mary, we both know Judas's dedication to Jesus. I have watched him grow into a man and into his faith. You are right to suspect Judas drank too much. We have all been under a great strain with the unrest in the city."

Uneasily, she said, "Of course, Peter can't be the one. Peter and his brother Andrew are devoted to Jesus. Rumors have it John the Baptist's teachings influenced both Peter and Andrew even before they met Jesus. Peter is always among the inner circle, and along with Andrew, one of the first called to follow Jesus."

"I've heard both Simon and Judas report many good things about the two of them. You know, it's said James and John have sought special positions of honor with Jesus. They are both fiery fanatics. Perhaps one of them is acting out of jealousy."

"Perhaps! But I cannot imagine either of them doing this. They are both zealous when it comes to discussing Jesus and his teachings. You know, Thomas seems the most doubtful of all the disciples. His perpetual questioning might lead him to do it."

"Yes! It has to be Thomas. Do you remember all the times Judas talked about how Thomas forever required more explanation? He seemed to need proof of Jesus' claims; as if miracles were not enough. And then there is Nathaniel, but I have not heard much about him.""

Amashia said, "Maybe so. I don't know much about Nathaniel either, but perhaps it's Matthew. After all, how could a tax collector be trusted? Maybe he is a spy for the Romans."

Before I could lay further blame on Thomas, an ominous knock on the door thudded through the hall. I looked at my friend, eyes fearful. I sensed something wrong, and I slowly rose from my chair. Zilpah, my maid, servant of many years, opened the door to Seth, our physician, neighbor, and good friend. He is much taller than most men are. On this day, he looked huge. As I looked into his normally compassionate eyes, I saw great pain.

"Mary," he hesitated, "May I come in?"

"It's Judas, isn't it?" I cried.

"Yes, Mary, it is. There is no easy way to tell you this. Judas hanged himself." His eyes did not meet mine; instead, they studied the spiral pattern on the tile floor, as if hopefully, it would spin him out of the room.

"No, no, no! This cannot be! This cannot be! Take me to him immediately!"

My scream of despair rang throughout my home.

Any thoughts of Amashia or concern for anything else were gone. I raced along following Seth, sobbing, swallowed up in agony over my last conversation with Judas. Seth and Amashia exchanged no words between them as they accompanied me. Tension wrapped like a tight woolen mantle around our hearts and strangled all conversation.

Finally, we arrived at the hateful site where Judas hanged himself. Judas chose the most desolate place at the edge of the city to end his life. He sought escape in the Hinnom Valley, a remote, rocky, and infertile area located outside the city. Citizens of Jerusalem avoided this tract of wasteland for fear of sliding down the steep walls of the valley onto the jagged rocks below.

I approached the spot where a frayed length of rope hung near the edge of a ravine. Judas's broken and contorted body lay far below, among the rocks at the bottom, the rest of the rope knotted around his neck. No one touched him because they did not want to go through a ritual of purification after attending to a dead body.

Seth said, "I need to leave you now and go to find your Simon. You need your husband here with you. Amashia, you take care of Mary, and I will return with Simon as soon as possible."

Frantically, I scrambled my way down the ravine to my son's body, dreadfully disfigured by the fall. Seeing his mangled body and the horrifying burns on his neck, I physically recoiled as my soul cried out in agony.

"Judas! Oh, my precious Judas! Why? Why?" My cries pierced the hideous sleeve of this awful place of damnation, and my wrenching sobs threatened to smother me. In the madness of my inconsolable grief, I wished myself dead also.

Yet, only then did I seriously consider the possibility Judas wasn't distraught or drunk, but telling me the truth when he spoke of betraying Jesus. My body collapsed in pain. My soul wailed, and my voice echoed it. Amashia told me later I sounded so painfully distraught any words I might have spoken were not discernible to her.

Sobbing uncontrollably, I mumbled, "Judas, Judas, I failed you when you came to me. I am so sorry. I could not bear to hear it. I did not listen. Forgive me! Forgive me!" Brokenly, I muttered, "I failed you miserably my son. Oh Judas, forgive me for not believing you! What have I done?"

With trembling hands, I brushed his curls from his face. My heart wrenched as I looked at his hair and beard matted with blood and debris. Gently, as if he could still feel my touch, I cleaned his face with my mantle. As I gazed upon his face, I noticed all the deep sadness had vanished. He found the peace in death he had not found in our last meeting. My tears fell upon his gentle face as I held him in my arms. My body bent over him, protecting him from the angry gazes from above. I wanted to shield and shelter him from what could not be undone.

The realization of Judas's crime and the consequences of my unwillingness to listen to him earlier were too much for me to bear. As I let the reality of what happened creep into my thoughts, something new occurred to me.

I cried out to God, "My Lord, my Lord. What has happened to Jesus?"

In panic, I shouted to no one, "What has happened to Jesus?"

"We don't know yet, Mary," Amashia replied.

Weeping, I knelt down beside the cold, grotesquely battered body of Judas. I cradled him in my arms and began to rock him back and forth, as if he were still a child. Stroking his forehead and hair, I whispered, "Judas, you didn't have to do this. Don't you know I still love you? I don't know why you chose to do what you did. I do know it will never change my love for you."

I heard a sound and looked up to see a small party approaching. Recognizing my husband, I mustered all the strength I possessed and reluctantly laid Judas's head on the harsh ground. I reached out to Simon, collapsing into his arms, but I received no comfort from him. His body containing no warmth, he became as cold and unfeeling as Judas's body.

"Simon ... what are we going to do? Judas came to me at an early hour and confessed he enabled the priest to take Jesus. I refused to believe him, Simon. I thought it drunken prattle."

Simon became enraged and flung me to the ground in front of him. I looked up feeling the same fear I felt when Judas left the upper room during the Passover meal the evening before. The father of our son and the loving husband I knew now gazed with loathing at our son.

Refusing to look at me, he said in a cold, callous voice, "Woman, you have failed as a mother. Your son has brought shame and disgrace to my house."

His words pierced my heart and an involuntary cry escaped my lips. "Must I lose both men I love so much this day?"

Simon, disgraced by his son's actions, spat at the corpse of his son. He raged at Judas; screaming, "How could you do this?"

Seth, and the men with him, glanced at each other, shook their heads knowingly, and acknowledged their friend's anger and grief as an expected reaction.

Seth reminded Simon, "You know Judas was repentant because he tried to return the thirty pieces of silver the Pharisees gave him. The priests refused to take the silver back. He must have realized what he had done could not be undone, or he would not have ended his life."

Simon, ignoring his friend's words of comfort, shouted, "Bury him right here, out of my sight and out of my memory! This act deserves no commemoration. I am going to find a gentile to dig his grave and lay him in it. None of us will go through the ritual of purification."

After his emphatic statement, Simon strode angrily away from us.

Seth said tenderly, "Mary, pay no attention to Simon's cruel words. He's not thinking about you. He is fearful about how he will face what Judas has done. He realizes he may not be accepted by either the priests or the followers of Jesus."

"But Seth, I have failed my son and my Lord. Simon is right."

Clearing his throat, Seth said, "Mary, as you know Simon and Judas went to the Temple last evening after they left the Passover celebration at Amashia's. I met up with them at the Temple. He knew Judas received the customary thirty pieces of silver for turning in a fellow Jew who had broken the law. Distraught, Simon tried to convince the Pharisees not to further break Jewish law by turning Jesus over to the Romans; gentiles no less! When Simon showed them their hypocrisy by breaking their own law of never turning a Jew over to a gentile, he ignited their vengeance. When Judas learned of the lawmakers' intentions, he went into deep remorse and bolted from the Temple knowing he was instrumental in breaking Jewish law. I don't think he expected this."

Amashia knelt beside me and said very softly, "Mary, Judas came to you out of remorse for what he had done. Nothing you could have done would have changed anything."

Her warm hand on my shoulder did not provide reassurance. Neither Amashia nor Seth's consoling words gave me comfort.

Simon returned with another man in tow, obviously a gentile. Without words, Simon pointed to the body of our son. The gentile began at a furious pace to dig a grave near Judas's remains.

With the grave barely opened, Simon ordered, "Throw the betrayer's body in the grave and cover him up."

After a pause, Simon began to speak again in a detached voice: "There will be no closing of the eyes, no washing of the body, no wrappings of perfumed cloth for this shameful act. There will be no wailings or flute players for you, Judas."

Simon grasped the left side of his garment and rent it across his body according to our custom. Without ceremony or public mourning, we buried our son.

I have no memory of leaving that bitter place. I vaguely remember Zilpah helping me to bed. Like my son lying in his shallow grave, I lay staring at the ceiling. No words escaped my lips to thank Zilpah, my maidservant who loved me and cared for me for years. The shame of Judas's act, the cruelty of my failure to listen to him, the shock of his hanging himself, and the staggering blow of my husband's turning away from me was more than I could bear.

Late in the day, Zilpah told me one of the Nazarenes brought the news about Jesus going before the Roman Governor, Pontius

Pilate. An act by default, he sentenced him to die by the most painful and degrading form of punishment known—crucifixion. The thought of our Lord subjected to such torture and pain cut me to the depths of my soul.

My mind, lost to reason and thought, a whole day and night passed before the world returned to me. Only then, did I rend my garment and turn it wrong side out in proper mourning. Simon, the servants, and I kept the tradition of not working for the next three days. Truly, we could not have done otherwise. We sat with our heads bound with sackcloth. Despair fogged my memory of those three days.

As we mourned Judas, we also awaited news of Jesus. Simon comforted himself by reading Lamentations aloud. My world, a world so perfect a few days earlier, had now become bleak and empty. A vast sea of shame separated me from my husband who had always been my protector. We did not speak, nor did we touch. Even our eyes sought out other sights to replace each other's face.

Zilpah entered my room and gently spoke.

"I overheard conversations between Simon and Seth. Mary, they have crucified Jesus. He is already laid in his tomb."

My shame forced me to hide my face so that even Zilpah could not see it.

I sobbed, "My Lord, my Lord, what have I done? If I had only listened to Judas, someone could have warned you. Oh, my Lord! I have lost my son, and now I have lost you. This is my fault!"

I felt responsible for the enormous loss, causing the destruction of the world as I knew it. This great tragedy spread over the land to all who knew Jesus. Bending to Hebrew custom,

I held myself accountable for the actions of my child. My soul withdrew from the light to an unknown place.

Seth returned late in the day to tell Simon the details of Jesus' death upon the cross. Seeing him enter the gate, I slipped quietly to a screen just outside the chamber where Simon received him. There I hid while I listened to his words.

"Before he died," Seth told Simon, "Jesus cried out, 'Father, forgive them, for they know not what they do.' Simon, listen to me," Seth continued, "Judas did not know all the ramifications of his deed. He may have thought he knew what the Pharisees would do, but he did not. Jesus prayed for Judas's forgiveness along with the others. Now, we must forgive Judas. Jesus asked God to forgive all those who sinned against him."

Simon's dark eyes seemed to look through Seth to a faraway place, and he did not respond. Forgetting the Lord's teaching of forgiveness, I filled my heart with self-blame and self-condemnation.

Seth explained, "Simon, many wondrous things happened while Jesus was suffering on the cross. The mystery of the darkness covering the sun was revealed when Jesus drew his last breath. Now we know why we had darkness for three hours in the middle of the day. During the same time, the curtain of the Temple split in two from top to bottom, the earth shook, and rocks split. God made his presence felt by everyone–believers and unbelievers alike."

I knew something was seriously wrong when the ground shook and day became night. God must have been expressing his sorrow through the unnatural elements of nature when Jesus died. In my sorrow and pain, I scarcely let it register in my mind. I could hardly stand to hear Seth, but neither could I stop listening.

Seth continued, "People were stunned to see even the long-dead walking the streets of Jerusalem. As I watched, even pagans were filled with awe at what they were seeing, confirming Jesus to truly be the son of God."

Seth's amazing reports about the crucifixion and the surrounding events astonished me. My shame still kept me hidden, so I strained to hear every word.

Zilpah came and stood behind me offering comfort as I listened to Seth and Simon.

"Mary, you could not have saved Jesus even if you listened to Judas before his death. You must understand it was already too late. My lady, you cannot carry the responsibility for the death of Jesus. The Pharisees, who are dedicated to uphold the Jewish law had already set Jesus' death in motion when Judas came to you. Their fear of the Jews from being led astray instigated this plot."

I found little solace in Zilpah's attempt to soothe me.

On the third day, Philip, one of the twelve, and the one closest to Judas, came to the house shouting, "He is not dead! He is not dead! Jesus is not dead! The stone rolled away. You must come! He is gone! He has risen."

Zilpah and Seth left with Philip to see this miracle.

"Not dead," I repeated to myself. *"I pray this is so, but it is unfathomable. After crucifixion, how can he not be dead? This is all too much for me to believe."*

I waited, hoping to get enough information to relieve my confusion and suffering.

Zilpah returned before the others in a state of excitement.

"Mary! The stone to Jesus' grave was rolled away. He is not there. He has since spoken to Mary Magdalene. Jesus is alive! We knew him to be a great prophet; now we have evidence. Mary, can you not see? You are relieved of responsibility for Jesus."

"Not responsible?" I thought, *"I gave birth to Judas. Judas, once so full of promise, now to be known forevermore as the betrayer. How could I, his mother, not be to blame?"* Rending my garment once more, I fell to my knees sobbing.

For days, neither Simon nor I left the house. Even so, we spoke no words to each other nor did our eyes meet. We moved quietly, like thieves in our own home. When guests came, I directed the servants to send them away. The house of Simon, once open to all who wished hospitality, now gave entrance to no one. It had become the tomb denied our son.

In torment, feeling rejected and admonished, I saw my husband turn his back to me, and heard his angry voice still clearly ringing out, "You have failed miserably as a mother. Your son has brought shame upon this house."

I kept repeating to myself, "If I had only listened."

Jesus is alive, but Judas is dead. What joy can there be for me? What I have done is too devastating. There is no life left for me.

Chapter 3

My son! My son! You were an extension of me; I felt your successes and your failures as my own. I failed you miserably, my son, and my heart is buried with you in sorrow. You were my greatest joy and my greatest blessing. All my life I knew I would have children. As a young girl, my father took a piece of wood and carved a baby for me. That little baby became my most prized possession. I would wrap the baby in a cloth and pretend to feed, bathe, and dress the baby, playing with him much of my day. Years later, when you were born, you became my life, just as the carved baby had been when I was a child. You were in my first thoughts *in the morning and in my final prayers at night. You were four years old before I let you out of my sight for more than a few moments.*

Oh Judas, you were a strong-willed little boy, able to do anything you set your mind to do. Stories about Moses fascinated you. You especially loved to hear about King David. I knew you would be a leader as I watched you pretend to be King David in your play. You grew from an imaginative, trusting child to become one of the most trusted followers of Jesus. When you first told me of your devotion to the Master, I was afraid you were deceived. When I learned more about Jesus and his teachings, my misgivings turned to pride because Jesus chose you to be among those closest to him. When you were chosen to serve God and the Messiah, what more could I have asked? What honor you brought to your father and me! If I had only listened to you when you came to me, you would be alive today. I am so ashamed. I cannot ask you to forgive me, Judas, as I cannot forgive myself.

That fateful day when this nightmare began, I awoke before dawn with a sense of foreboding. My heavy heart held hope Judas would be home for our Passover celebration and yet, I had a nagging feeling in my stomach — a forewarning of something terribly wrong. I tried to assure myself, *we have always been together for this most important of our High Holy Days.* Assured I was not! As fear raced through my body, I asked aloud, "Where is this fear coming from? Why am I feeling so forlorn?" Hoping to get an answer, I was shaken, unable to discern what troubled me. My thoughts turned to all the rumors, rumblings, and unrest among those who doubted the Master. I thought about how his teachings upset the foundational beliefs of the Scribes and Pharisees so much they constantly tested him, hoping to prove him false. As I recalled all I had heard about the high priest trying to turn the people against Jesus, I finally identified my fear — *fear my only son, Judas would not be home to celebrate this Passover with us.* My heart raced as I sensed Jesus and his twelve, Judas among them, could be in danger. I attempted to shake these feelings by remembering the joy of previous Passover celebrations. The joys of the past could not help me find joy this morning. My sense of anxiety prevented me from completing my morning prayers. My mind finally turned to all the preparations needed for this most Holy Day. My heartbeat quickened as I arose from my mat. I saw the faintest pink line of dawn through my high window as I hurriedly folded my mat and placed it near my favorite chest. Moving to the chest Simon had given me at Judas's birth, I ran my hands over the beautiful carvings as I had done so many times. Hoping for comfort, I gently traced the intricate olive garden scene on the front of the chest.

Pulling my finest indigo tunic from the chest, I dressed for the day, carefully choosing my clothes in honor of Passover. I selected a veil to match my tunic. These loose fitting garments slid easily over my thin body. I completed my attire with an elaborately embroidered girdle. My mind continued to whirl with the rumors and murmurings prevalent throughout Jerusalem. My hands trembled as I braided my long graying hair. I tried to recall the teachings of the Master hoping to find peace and blot out my anxiety.

At first, we had called this humble man "Rabbi," but the first time I heard him teach, I sensed he just might be the promised one. More than once I had heard him say, "Do not worry about the details of your life." Yet, on this morning, I could not find peace from his words.

I needed the strength and reassurance his wisdom would

provide, and being in his presence gave me more strength and comfort than I had experienced. Such pride I felt to know Jesus chose our son to serve not only as his treasurer, but also as one of his disciples. He never strayed far from Jesus' side. Judas's devotion to Jesus turned to a passionate obsession. Judas was radiant as he spoke of the kingdom Jesus would establish. My heart overflowed with joy and satisfaction in the role my son played in Jesus' ministry.

The lingering peals of a distant bell rang from the center of the city, calling the city to waking prayers, and rousing me from my reverie. I placed the veil on my head and wound it loosely over my shoulders, completing my dress for the day.

Quietly, I slipped into the room where my husband Simon lay peacefully sleeping. In the faint light of dawn, he looked as he had the first morning I woke to see him as my husband. The curls lay on his forehead in disarray hiding the gray in his hair. I remembered coming to him as a young bride, my heart full of hope and determined to become the best of wives and earn his love. Pride swelled in my breast when I thought of his knowledge of our Hebraic law and his teachings in the temple. The Priests and Scribes received him with deference, and many came from great distances to listen to him interpret the law. I felt honored he had chosen me to bear his son.

Simon's wealth and education commanded a place of respect wherever he went. Even after many years of marriage, I was still in awe of him. His steadfast devotion to family and friends became the rock stabilizing my life. No day passed I didn't thank God for the opportunity to manage a household strictly obedient to God's law. I felt a sense of comfort as I gazed at his resting form. I knelt and laid my head on his chest.

Awakening, Simon drew me close. Then, realizing the significance of the day, playfully, he admonished me, "Mary! Have you forgotten today is a very busy day? You have chores for the Passover feast, and I must go to the Temple to assist with the sacrifices and sacred rituals. Why are you wasting time dallying with your husband?"

"If you would only wake and rise immediately, I would not be tempted to spend the day dawdling," I responded in jest. Simon yawned and grunted as he rubbed his face and eyes and placed his hand upon my shoulder as he rose. I folded his mat and placed it in the highly polished chest in the corner of the room. He began pouring water into the basin and splashing it about. As he bathed, I laid out a simple tunic for him to wear to breakfast. Side by side, with careful attention to every detail, I placed the undergarment, the tunic, and the many-colored girdle he would wear to the Temple. Simon, a very particular man about his appearance, allowed me the wifely pleasure of placing each item in perfect order for him.

Simon quickly completed his bathing and donned his tunic. We walked to the great room where we usually took our meals. He seated himself on a thick rug beside a low table. Then I followed the aromas coming from the kitchen and fetched his breakfast. Zilpah, our beloved servant and companion since before Judas's birth, had the food waiting on a tray. Serving Simon the tea and warm bread Zilpah prepared, I stepped behind him, waiting in silence, ready to return to the kitchen for more food or tea if he should wish it. This day was too important for Simon to remain silent. He wanted to share his thoughts with me before he faced the throngs at the Temple. He patted the rug at his feet, and as I sat, he began to talk.

Simon asserted, "I am uncomfortable about the unrest at the Temple. I am anxious to get there this morning to see what is happening. I hope to get news of Judas today."

"Simon, I greatly want to see Judas this evening. Perhaps Jesus will share this feast with us. Oh, Simon! How blessed we would be if we could hear him teach here in our home!"

Simon's face reflected the fleeting darkness. He did not respond to my enthusiastic comment, but turned to the unrest between the Priests and Scribes. "Mary, there are many who doubt Jesus is the Messiah. The Scribes and Pharisees are condemning him to everyone who will listen. Some have even threatened his followers. Argument and distrust dominate the daily discussions among the men at the Temple."

My throat tightened at the mention of threats. Realizing the strictness of the Scribes and Pharisees and the importance of Simon's role among them, the fear returned for his safety and the safety of our son.

"Some say Jesus is a prophet." Simon continued, "Others say he is a charlatan who has taken advantage of his relationship with John the Baptist. There are even those who say he is a cheap magician who duped the masses. Several of the influential priests believe he has come to destroy the orderly rites of the Temple. Some seem jealous of the devotion of the crowds toward him and openly ridicule the reports of his miracles."

Simon had never before revealed to me the depth of his concern for what he had seen and heard, and my anxiety grew as I quietly thought about what he had said. After a while, I asked, "Simon, what are you saying? What do you think will happen?"

"I am worried the Scribes and Pharisees are so threatened, they may want to take Jesus' life."

Hearing this made my heart race. Quickly, I dismissed his words, not wanting to consider them. "Today is Passover. Let us not think of danger and intrigue, Simon. I feel certain we will see Judas and have more insight before the night falls. It has been too long since we shared a meal with our beloved son. He has been out of the city with Jesus for several moons." I could hardly wait for his laughter to fill our home once more. "What a celebration we will have," I consoled myself. "He will have stories to tell of the miracles he has seen and stories of his time spent with Jesus."

The meal finished, Simon rose and reached for my hand, saying, "Mary, do not be disappointed if we do not hear anything. I am confident Judas is fine." We walked together to his room, where he would dress for the day.

As I tended to my husband's grooming and dress, I mused over the similarity of Judas to his father. Both men, taller than most, moved with dignity. Their dark skin and curly hair gave them an appealing softness of expression. Both Judas and Simon were slow to smile, but when they did, their faces lit up like the morning sun. The most remarkable resemblance in their smile delighted me. With the grace of educated men, they were able to reach out to people from all backgrounds and from all lands. Sometimes it surprised me how stubborn and unyielding they both could be when they believed in the correctness of their actions. They shared a determined nature and a passion for the work of the one true God.

I remembered Simon's many reservations when Judas first told us about following Jesus. He respected Judas's decision. If he had doubts, he kept all concerns hidden in his heart out of respect for his son. As he preformed his daily duty in the Temple, he never entered into the criticism of Jesus, or his teachings. Yet,

I understood his need not to upset either the Pharisees or the followers of Jesus. Picking sides would endanger the position he loved so well.

Simon donned his white linen drawers with some awkwardness, and I smiled as he struggled, drawing my mind back to the present. I held his checkered tunic as he slipped into it. He wrapped the colorful girdle several times around his still-slender waist and arranged the folds to reach to the hem of his garment. I could see that his mind was occupied with the solemn rites of Passover and the unrest recently permeating the Temple.

My anxiety returned after Simon left in haste to get to the temple. With great effort, I forced myself to turn my attention to the many tasks involved in preparing for the Passover feast. I hurried to the kitchen to join my servants in the day's tasks. Zilpah waited for me to direct her duties. Perhaps I could lose myself in the myriad of simple tasks of the household and regain some of the excitement of previous feast days.

I remembered when Judas first became a follower of Jesus. It occurred to me Jesus could be a false prophet. Only after getting to know the Master and his teachings, did my misgivings turn to pride knowing my only son was among those closest to him. As keeper of the purse, Judas held the responsible position of accounting for every coin received and spent wisely. How thrilling to be selected to serve God and the Messiah! What honor, Judas brought us, his father and mother!

I was overjoyed when Judas made sure Simon and I knew the times Jesus was teaching at a distance where we could go to hear him. Because of this, I heard Jesus' teachings on many occasions. Unlike others who interpreted the laws strictly, Jesus welcomed women and spoke to them directly. His eyes sought out women and men equally as he taught.

My heart filled to overflowing when Jesus spoke to me! How full of joy the household became when his laughter and gentle bantering rang out! He truly brought happiness and light wherever he went. My hand went to my left shoulder, as I remembered how he had placed his own hand there. He looked so deeply into my eyes I knew he saw into my very soul. I was never the same. I became certain Jesus was the Son of God. I thanked God again for my own precious son who brought all these blessings to me.

The sounds of voices coming through the kitchen door interrupted my prayers. The voices were those of my dear friend, Amashia, and her servants. Amashia was ample in size and much taller than the rest of the women in the kitchen. She had a penchant for vibrant colored clothing, matching her robust personality. Her bold and spirited speech assured me of her nearness. Physically, we were a contrast in size. I being short and small; she being tall and robust. We were a sight when seen walking together. Still, we were ideally matched as teachers. We followed our tradition, serving as teachers of the younger women at the Temple. After her husband's untimely death, Amashia stepped in and carried on her husband's business, making her truly unique among women.

As Amashia entered the kitchen, her hearty laughter filled the house, and I joined her even though I did not know the basis of her happiness. "Come, my dearest friend, and tell me the source of your good humor today," I beckoned her.

Amashia smiled cheerfully in response. The large kitchen seemed to shrink as she entered, laden with baskets. Also carrying large baskets covered with linen cloths, her two servants were close behind her. Taking a basket from one of her servants and placing it on the nearest bench, she heaved a sigh of relief and said, "I brought cakes of figs for you and your guests." Peering inside, I saw fig, pomegranate, and date delicacies. Just as Zilpah and I had so eagerly anticipated Judas's presence tonight, so did dear Amashia.

The heat of the kitchen drove us into the garden. We sat under the shade of an olive tree and exchanged our mutual plans for Passover. The fragrance of the exotic flowers Simon loved filled the air. He would buy every rare plant from traveling caravans visiting the market. This garden magnified the beauty of our home. Amashia and I had spent many enthralled hours under this tree discussing all the news we learned of Jesus' miraculous work. We were enthralled, mystified and excited by Jesus, his works, and his teachings.

Looking around the garden, Amashia grew quiet for a moment and looked up wistfully. As she picked up a flower and studied it, she said, "My husband, Tahan, and I shared so many happy times in our garden, and being in this lovely place always brings back those memories."

My heart drifted back to the tragedy that befell Tahan four years ago. He had been traveling with a merchant caravan when a member of the party fell from his horse severely injuring him. Tahan had ridden on alone to seek help. A group of caravan raiders attacked and killed him. Shocked, the entire community mourned along with Amashia.

"Amashia," I said, "I know you must miss Tahan, especially at this holy time."

"Yes, I do," Amashia, responded sadly. "But Mary, I will always remember how you helped me through the times following Tahan's death. I don't know how I would have ever gotten through it without you." I reached for her and held her close. In our silence, I felt the closeness of our bond.

After a few moments I said, "Amashia, Tahan would be very proud of the way you rose up and continued to conduct his business. You chose a fine way to honor what you had together. His wealth has multiplied, and you have shared it as generously as he would have. The two of you were perfectly suited."

"You are right, Mary. That's why I miss him so."

"We all sorely miss him." Taking her hand, I said, "Your faith, your hospitality, and your generosity have blessed us all. You have wonderful memories of him as a loving father and husband who held fast to God's laws."

"I am grateful to have such wonderful memories."

"Amashia, you have filled your days with God's work. Your example as a true believer in Jesus is a light to all who know you. You have made it possible for your household to hear the Teacher speak, and they have taken him into their hearts." Amashia, with characteristic humility, passed her hand over her face as if to lower her veil and close the topic. She began to discuss the upcoming feast.

"Where do you think Jesus and his inner circle will take the Passover feast? Have you had word from Judas yet? Surely, he will find a way to spend this Holy Day with us." She did not wait for replies, but kept up pleasant chatter as she plucked an especially beautiful blossom and held it close to relish its fragrance.

"Amashia," I said, suddenly becoming serious, "I have a strange foreboding I do not fully understand. I woke up with the feeling this morning and cannot rid myself of it."

Amashia leaned down toward me and lowered her voice to avoid even trusted servants hearing her. "Mary, have you heard what the priests at the Temple are plotting against Jesus? Rumor has it they are fearful he will upset the Romans and bring Rome's wrath upon us all. Do you think Herod knows many of us believe Jesus came to lead us out of oppression? I am very uneasy concerning Jesus' safety."

"I am too," I said. "I just haven't wanted to admit my worry."

With a glance at the sun, Amashia quickly rose from the bench. "Look at you," she demanded, attempting to squelch our fretfulness. "Keeping me away from my household duties on such a busy day! What kind of a friend are you, Mary? Can it be you are better prepared than I for this High Holy Day?"

Returning to practical matters dispelled the heaviness of the previous moment. "Amashia, no one will be better prepared than you."

"I must gather my chattering servants and hurry home. There is still brass to polish, mats to spread, and water to be stored to wash the feet of weary travelers who may come to my door. I need two sets of hands to prepare everything properly in time." She laughed at herself with the last comment and quickly pulled her veil over her face. With one last affectionate hug, she called to her servants and hurried out the garden gate. I returned to my kitchen, trying to reassure myself there was nothing to worry about.

Zilpah met me at the door, holding a large wooden bowl filled with finely ground wheat. With an attempt to get over my apprehension, I told Zilpah I would prepare the bread for our Passover feast making sure it would be unleavened, not permitted to rise. The clay ovens were hot and ready for the bread. Both of us stood nearby and kept watchful eyes as the bread baked. It was important for the bread to be a perfect batch as important guests might join our household tonight. I still hoped our son would be home, and perhaps Jesus' presence would grace our home too. We prepared twelve cakes, covered them with linen napkins, and placed them in baskets before they were stored on the kitchen benches. Other baskets filled quickly as we carefully placed the thin flat bread in them.

We had just finished the task when one of Amashia's menservants raced through the kitchen garden. Out of breath, he excitedly said, "Ma'am, my mistress sends you news. Jesus and his chosen twelve are taking the Passover meal at her house tonight. She would like you to bring your food to the house of Tahan. She urges you to hurry, for she needs you to help her make ready."

Zilpah and I just looked at each other with an unspoken question. *Was Judas not coming home to us?* Despite my disappointment, I set the servants busy gathering food to take on the trip to Amashia's kitchen. By the time Zilpah and I had fastened our veils, the preparations were ready. "Zilpah," I said, "Ask your son to stay behind until everyone knows where we will be taking our meal tonight. Make sure everyone knows they are welcome." We set out with many questioning glances flying between us. We chose the back way because even at this hour the streets overflowed with people and animals.

Once we were on the upper path, lowing cattle, bleating sheep, and the jabbering of human voices filled the air. A sea of humanity covered by a cloud of dust surged toward the Temple on the road below. Shouts from those herding the animals mingled with the laughter and loud voices of pilgrims. So many people had come to sacrifice and take part in the holy rites. Among the drab tunics of the poor were bright specks of color as wealthy pilgrims were borne on litters. The scene so fascinated Zilpah I had to pull her along by her arm to get her feet moving toward higher ground. In the distance, the Temple glittered in the blazing rays of the sun, as if to draw the people to their destination on the billowing cloud of dust. The air seemed full of strangeness, and questions seemed to hammer through my mind. My body shuddered with nervousness engulfing me. Somewhere in the deep recesses of my soul, I knew this Passover would be very, very different.

✧

Chapter 4

Amashia's home was located some distance from us, on a higher level of the city. We hurried along the back paths ordinarily used by servants as they went about their errands. As we passed Herod's palace, its beauty and opulence caused all of us to slow our pace. We never grew weary of taking in the magnificent surroundings. We gazed in awe at the graceful bronze statues from where water poured. Circular porticoes and walkways surrounded the palace. Canals and gardens created a different scene out of every walkway, while exotic plants and animals ornamented each area. I thought, *"Herod has surrounded himself with the beauty of everything conceivable, including his wife Miriamme. Can a man of such excellent taste also be as evil as men say?"*

We increased our pace after we passed the palace and were soon entering Amashia's kitchen where we found her nervously fanning herself.

Approaching Amashia, I said, "Why are you so flustered? You have entertained many guests of great importance without such upheaval. What is so different? Surely you know the Master will accept whatever you offer him?"

Amashia turned to me with a faraway look in her eyes, slowly replying, "You speak the truth; however, the circumstance surrounding the news of his arrival is very unusual. Let me tell you how I found out he and his twelve were to be my guests."

"Please do," I countered, curiosity piqued. I had never seen Amashia so agitated over entertaining. Questions tumbled about my head as the two of us rose and began to walk around the room, carefully assuring ourselves all was ready for the Passover guests.

Amashia continued, "This morning before coming to your house, I took all the women of the household to the well for water. We placed water in the urns near the door to wash our guests' feet as well as in the lower and upper rooms for cleansing at mealtime. We had brought enough water for everyone." Amashia stopped walking and looked at the urns sitting at each end of the room as though they might disappear.

After a few moments of studying the urns and the room in general, Amashia looked back at me and continued, "The cooks came to me after midday saying we needed more water. Every woman in the household was very busy, so I sent Zeb to the well with a large water pot. He grumbled about doing women's work, but went his way. When he returned, his excitement affected his speech making him difficult to understand." Again, Amashia turned and examined the chamber where we stood.

"Zeb filled his large water pitcher at the well. John and Peter approached Zeb as he began to walk away. They explained Jesus had sent them to find a man carrying a pitcher of water and to follow him home. Once there, they were to tell the householder, 'Our teacher asks you show us your upper room where he will eat the Passover meal with his disciples.' Once they had examined the upper chamber, they departed to tell Jesus all was arranged."

Clapping my hands in amazement, I said, "How like the Master! They did not know in whose home they would celebrate the Passover. You have received a great honor. I can understand your excitement."

Shaking her head pensively, Amashia said, "Jesus requests he sup alone with his twelve. I know you were hoping to spend this evening with your son. So, Mary, you may stay behind the screen in the upper room and oversee all their needs. I will give you two young men to fetch the requirements of those present. This will allow you to be near Judas and to serve our master at the same time. I will take care of our guests downstairs." Her countenance brightened at the rightness of her decision. I smiled. Amashia's enthusiasm was always contagious. At first I was disappointed, because I desperately longed to be with my son face to face. Even so it was better to see him and be in the same room with him—even though he would not see me—than not to be with him at all this night.

Between us, we were sure we had more than enough food prepared. The unblemished male lamb Zeb had selected days before roasted over the coals. The savory aroma wafted into the kitchen and mingled with the fragrant spices and breads. The large open fire chamber held numerous cooking pots, bubbling and steaming. Surely, we had prepared enough food to feed half of Jerusalem! The bitter herbs and salt had been prepared and placed on different tables in the house. Artfully arranged, woven trays of dried figs and grapes had already been placed on the long, low tables in both the upper and lower chambers. Shallow, decorated bowls of olives soaked in vinegar and oil were scattered about the table. Bowls for cleansing of the hands were in place on stands. Cups to hold wine waited for filling from large pitchers. To make the guests comfortable, the servants carefully placed thick mats for reclining without any crowding.

In the upper chamber, luxury emanated with the finest of linen cloths draping the long table. Divans graced the walls on three sides of the richly carved table. Cushions embroidered in bright colors made the divans inviting to weary travelers. On the wide window ledge sat two large water pots, a deep wooden bowl, and towels. Sweet blossoms below the open windows filled the room with faint perfume. Preparations were made ready for a king. Our dear Lord would surely find comfort here tonight with his beloved companions.

My thoughts turned again to my son Judas. How I longed to talk with him and to hear his deep voice. I needed to know how things were with him. When I closed my eyes, I envisioned Judas as he had looked when he met Jesus. I could see his strong, muscular body dressed in the rich tunics and robes appropriate for a prominent merchant. How I had enjoyed embroidering those ornate mantles! When he decided to follow Jesus, he gladly put aside his fine clothing and wore the simple tunic of the common traveler. I remembered his excitement as he told me of Jesus, the one of whom the prophets spoke.

I knew he would be dressed much more poorly and would likely need barbering after all the months on the road; yet in my vision, Judas looked as meticulously groomed as ever. I knew nothing could dim the bright light of passion in Judas's eyes. I recalled seeing the passion in his eyes when he spoke to his father and me about the day Jesus would make his divine leadership known to all. His eyes shone with a strange light as tears of joy spilled down his cheeks. At the time, before I got to know Jesus, I thought Judas had gone mad. Some, like James and John, were concerned with their position in the new kingdom. Judas's main concern was for Jesus to declare his kingdom.

The high voice of the boy at the gate pierced the air and roused me from my thoughts. "Jesus comes! They come! Make ready!" He jumped to the ground from his perch on the gatepost and swung the gate wide. Jesus, appearing weary from travel, entered a few steps ahead of the others. He looked deeply into each person's eyes along the path and embraced them before moving forward. Occasionally, he would stop to speak to one of the guests before approaching the next one. While he physically had no beauty or majesty to attract us to him, he aroused strong emotion in all present just as he had when he taught the multitudes. The awe we held for him radiated from each face of those present. Every guest and servant glowed with the anticipation of being able to touch him and to be near him. Jesus' smile broadened as he bent forward to kiss the children while they hugged his knees.

Delayed, the rest of the party entered two and three at a time calling out greetings as they walked up the pathway. Judas came last. A frown clouded his face and he stared at the ground. Only when I ran to him and knelt at his side, did he appear to become animated. He soon joined in with the others in the mood of the occasion.

Wanting to receive his blessing and to show him the openness of my heart, I held up my palms to him. Judas reached down, pulled me to my feet. Without words, he held me close to his heart. His emotions were so strong he could find no words to greet me. He held me and began to sway back and forth. When he finally held me away from him, I trembled looking at his thin face and sunburned skin. He did not look like the son of a successful Scribe and merchant. He appeared more like a simple farmer or herdsman. He wore a simple robe of rough cloth sorely in need of a good washing. The only sign of being an important man in Jesus' inner circle was the fine leather purse held tightly to his waist by strong straps. No outward appearances could put out the fire burning in his eyes. After another kiss of greeting, we joined the others.

There we found Amashia, greeting each guest by bowing and then touching her forehead, lips, and heart meaning, "My mind, my words, and my heart are here to serve you." She assured all present her house was their house. When Jesus approached her, he held both her hands and then placed his right hand on her head, saying, "Peace to you and your household. This day you are a servant of God's will." He then went to each servant, blessing and touching each face tenderly. The room became quiet, and all gazed lovingly at this man unlike any other. His very presence brought a sense of peace to all of us. He glowed with a power beyond my comprehension. The adoration of him by all in the household was apparent.

For reasons I could not fathom, my throat ached with tears, and it took all my strength to remain at Amashia's side. I wanted desperately to be alone with Judas. He did not seem like himself. He seemed distant and chose to avoid close contact with anyone. Seeing my son like this only heightened the unease I had felt all day.

Servants quickly bathed the feet of our honored guests. The dust of the roads clung to their weary feet and they gratefully received the soothing coolness of the water. Jesus surprised all present by taking a small flask from Zeb's hand, containing precious perfumed oil reserved for the most important visitors in the home, while thanking them for the opportunity to serve his party's needs, Intrigued, we watched Jesus perform this kindness. Jesus went to each servant, anointing them with oil.

Servants then led the guests to quarters where they could bathe and rest briefly before gathering for the Passover feast. Amashia reassured Jesus only he and his followers would feast in the upper room. She would guard their privacy. He smiled graciously and thanked her. He again repeated, "This day you are a servant of God's will."

As the guests retired to ready themselves for the evening meal, the household returned to the remaining, numerous small tasks. A happy harmony among the household made the tasks enjoyable. Amashia and I held each other's hands and congratulated ourselves for our readiness. Laughter bubbled up from Amashia's deep bosom as she admonished me, "Are you sure you can remember to feed all the guests? I saw your eyes, and they never left Judas's face. He no longer looks like a pampered youth. His days on the roads with our Messiah have made a man of him. Be proud! Of course when he gets his beard properly trimmed he will look more like himself." I had nearly forgotten my feelings of tearfulness. Amashia always made my heart lighter with just the right words.

Chapter 5

When the hot sun dropped below the horizon, the ram's horn sounded the time for evening prayers. In the softest twilight, the evening's gathering swelled as other people began to arrive. Jesus and the disciples mounted the stairway to the upper room for the Passover meal. I stood behind the latticed screen in the hallway with two young serving boys and carefully counted each entrant into the upper room. Once everyone had entered, I sent the first boy in with the best wine we had to offer. The thick walls muted the deep voices of thirteen men; yet singing of ancient hymns of thanksgiving seeped through to me.

Being careful not to be seen, I looked through small openings from behind the screen at the room before me to be sure all lamps were full and burning brightly, looking at each couch to be sure pillows were in place. As the serving boy entered the room, a general disruption among Jesus' twelve followers arose. As usual, each one hoped to sit beside Jesus. Jesus called the youngest disciple, Mark, to his side. Jesus glanced around the room, his eyes resting on Peter whom he waved to the couch on his other side. All of them having hoped for the honor grumbled a bit, chose a couch, and settled in. Judas sat looking directly at Jesus. Being careful to remain unseen, I could see the serving boy standing patiently with the first wine. To everyone's surprise, Jesus did not call for the wine. Instead, he stood and removed his outer garment and tied up his girdle.

I could not believe my eyes as he took a clean towel and walked toward a nearby brass basin filled with water. He lifted it and placed it on the floor in front of one of the twelve. He knelt before each one and bathed their feet. As he washed their feet, he said, "I serve you in love as you will serve others. When I am no longer with you, remember, even the most humble act of kindness done in my name, is the greatest honor to God, the Father."

At Jesus' statement, the men fell silent. Low murmurs buzzed around the room, but none moved from his place. I could not hear what they were saying, yet I could not drop my gaze. As Jesus came to each man, he looked at him with love and yet, with great sadness. As he neared Judas, Judas sat up straighter and taller. I sensed he dreaded Jesus' serving him in such a lowly way. When I gazed at Judas's face, I could not guess his thoughts. He scowled, and for a moment, I thought he would bolt from the room. However, Jesus sat near him; Jesus reached to touch the sleeve of Judas as if to tell him something. The Master continued the washing of the feet, moving from man to man, until he served every man. Jesus stood; set the basin aside, dried his hands, and again put on his outer garment. He returned to his place at the table.

Jesus said the blessing in accordance with the ancient ritual, and the first wine was served. He spoke in a voice somber, but loud enough for all to hear. "This is my last meal with you, for I must fulfill the prophecy of old. As you drink this wine, drink it as my blood. It is a testament of the blood I shall shed for you." He sipped from the cup and passed it to Mark. The room fell completely silent. My mind whirled. I could not understand why he would call the wine "blood." I wondered if the twelve hushed disciples knew.

Jesus then took a thin piece of the unleavened bread, and again he gave the ritual blessing and thanked God for the deliverance of the Jews. He said, "As you eat of this bread, it is my body I sacrifice for you. Celebrate our people's deliverance by sharing this bread among you. I shall not drink again of the vine until the kingdom of God shall come."

As he looked into the hearts of each one, he said, "Drink, all of you, even the one who will betray me, for he sits boldly among us. He shares my love and my meal, yet he shares not in the kingdom."

At this pronouncement, the men raised their voices in protest, and my stomach knotted, as the cold feeling of fear I had been battling all day returned in full force. The disciples adamantly denied the possibility of having a traitor among them. Each man protested his innocence. Jesus shook his head as if they were children. His penetrating gaze quieted their cries. Again, he said, "I tell you once more, one of you who sits with me tonight shall betray me. It is one who dips into this dish with me."

As silence and despair filled the room, he continued, "The Son of man must leave you as it is written, but woe unto the one who betrays the Son. It would be better for him if he were never born. I know who it is, and I can look into his heart. In my death, all will remember my life. None will forget the one whose faith failed thus fulfilled the prophecy."

Looking around the room, I felt certain none of these men could lose their faith. The men's voices rose in argument with him as they loudly proclaimed their undying loyalty. Each man shouted his willingness to give his life for the Master. Jesus said, "Do not make our final hours together dark with dissension." With these words, he began to sop the bread. He then turned and gave Peter the first sop from the bowl.

Peter looked at Jesus with a petulant expression. "I have never doubted you. My loyalty is above question." Jesus touched his face gently and answered, "Satan would have taken you from me long ago had I not prayed to my Father in Heaven that your faith would not fail."

Peter, once again, loudly denied that he would ever falter in supporting Jesus.

Though the righteous desires tried Jesus' patience, he still spoke with kindness to Peter. "I tell you now you will deny me three times this night before the morning cock crows."

Peter shook his head vehemently. "Never, never!" he cried.

The disciples looked at each other and wondered, for among the twelve, none had shown his devotion more readily than Peter. Tears came from Peter's eyes and fell upon Jesus' hand.

He said, "Dear Master, I would follow you even to prison or to death. My love for you is here for all to see."

Jesus smiled sadly. "My death, which is imperative, will harden your faith. As a result of these trials, you will grow in faith and carry on my work."

At this, Peter fell to his knees placing his head against the master's side, crying out, "I swear I shall never forsake you. I would surrender my life before I would turn my back on you."

Jesus reached down and gently pulled Peter back to his seat. His gentle smile calmed all of the men at the table as he urged them, "Let us get on with this holy feast."

Solemnly, Jesus told the ancient story of God's angels bringing death to the first born of Egypt and of God's hand forcing the pharaoh to let his people go to their own land. He spoke of Moses and Aaron, and a look of joy crossed his face as he recounted the miracles of old. He again reminded the disciples of Moses' devotion and patience, and then he prayed for them and all those who were engaged in the honored traditions of this Holy Day. As he ended his prayer, he looked through the nearby window to the heavens. He seemed to be speaking to someone just outside: "Oh, Lord, please be near me. If it be thy will, help me in my salvation. Touch my heart and make me strong that thy will be done."

His prayer puzzled me. My mind went in circles, and my heart felt heavy in my chest. Turning my gaze toward each man, I asked myself which of these men whom I so admired would not stand for Jesus.

"Of course, it could not be Judas. Judas, who had such devotion and fire each time he spoke of the coming kingdom. He saw Jesus as a

43

mighty king. He would never betray our Master," I thought. When I looked at Judas, he looked down, and his hand covered part of his face. Did he know the man who would betray our Messiah? His distress was evident in the tense position of his body and the scowl on his face. I felt sadness for all of the disciples. Moreover, I felt especially anxious for my son who so eagerly waited for the Messiah's return to his rightful throne.

The men continued to discuss Jesus' words, each deeply troubled by the mysterious message. One by one, the disciples asked Jesus, "Is it I?"

Jesus, as always, had compassion for them. He responded by quoting the prophets of old, "Surely you remember the ancient scriptures handed down to you, "If you think it good, give me my price, and if not, forbear. They weighed for my price thirty pieces of silver, and the Lord said unto me, cast it unto the potter. And I took the thirty pieces of silver and I cast them to the potter in the house of the Lord."

Plainly, the scriptures did not enlighten the apostles any more than they enlightened me. Even when Jesus knew death could come at any hour, he spoke to his followers with puzzling words. He stood and began to move around the room, now a chamber of confusion and sorrow.

Jesus neared Nathanial, who spoke up and said, "Master, do you remember our first meeting and you said to me, 'Behold, an Israelite in whom there is no guile.'" Nathanial's voice rang out as he recounted the event, "Immediately I confessed my faith, saying, 'You are the Son of God. You are the king of Israel.'" Nathanial reached out to Jesus, touching his garment and wailing, "Truly it cannot be I!"

Tears filled my eyes as I saw the anguish on Jesus' face. He did not answer in words; rather he clasped Nathanial's hands in his. He walked to Matthew, the tax collector. I wondered; *"Could this be the one? The one so many despise?"* Jesus took the hand of Matthew and held it to his lips. Closing his eyes, Jesus kissed Matthew's fingertips. Before slowly walking to James, Jesus without words, had reassured Matthew. James pleaded in a loud voice, "Surely it is not I? I have believed that since the day I saw John baptize you. I saw the Holy Spirit descend upon you. I have walked every step with you. It cannot be I, my Lord."

Jesus put his hands upon James' head and whispered a prayer I could not hear. James quietly bowed his head. Jesus continued until he had touched each of the disciples. Each of them proclaimed their love and devotion as he came near them. When he came to my dear Judas, he stopped and gazed at him. Time stood still for me.

He leaned toward Judas and in a voice choked with emotion said to him, "Go and do what you must do. Go quickly!"

Judas stood and swiftly left the room.

I stepped from behind the screen and reached out to my son, but he brushed me aside. I called out his name. He turned back. The turmoil in his eyes frightened me. He said, "Not now, mother! I have a task to do."

"God be with you," I said to him as he descended the stairs. I thought, *Jesus must have sent him on a special mission. He has entrusted him with an errand he cannot share with the others."* Even as this thought settled in my mind, I had an ominous feeling. Judas's face did not look as if he were on a joyous mission. In fact, he looked fearful. I shivered, even in the warm evening.

I prayed Judas would not fall into the hands of the evil Romans or the doubting men at the Temple. He frequently visited those doubters when in Jerusalem because of his father Simon, an influential man in those quarters. Judas came and went as he always had, and I knew the priests questioned him on each visit. He often complained of the endless questions and the whining fear of those old men. No miracle ever quite inspired the Pharisees' belief in the Messiah. Judas's well-known eloquence had not swayed them from their quarrelsome disputes, and Simon's fear expressed just this morning returned to haunt me. I hid myself in the shadows and forced the trembling of my body to cease.

Soon the serving boys took away the remains of the meal while Jesus and the remaining eleven men washed their hands and quietly rose from their couches. Once more Jesus prayed. Again, the disciples began to question who would betray him.

Peter, the most boisterous, complained, "When you speak of betrayal, you cast doubts and discord among us. Name this betrayer so we may drive him away. We must stand as one in the face of the Roman enemy. Who is this traitor?"

Jesus holding his empty palms upward toward the group said, "My brothers, any one of you could have betrayed me, for all of you are captivated by your own desires. All are weak without the power of our heavenly Father, but one of you has a burning obsession, and cannot love those who are not among the chosen people."

I pondered the words of Jesus, as did the disciples. I believed with all my heart that the Jews were especially blessed people. After all, we are God's chosen ones, and Jesus' teachings of the equality of God's love were unsettling to all of us. Somehow, I felt the gentiles could not be as dear to God as his own people could. Even so, Jesus repeated the message he had diligently delivered everywhere he went. "God made men in his own image and loves all those whom he created."

My mind wandered back to all the times I saw him reach

out to the women and teach them alongside their husbands and sons. He treated us with as much dignity and respect as he did the men. No other religious leader had ever included women in the same manner as men.

No bounds to his loving kindness existed. Many were astonished when he reached out to the prostitutes. Lepers, tax collectors, common and noble men were all the same in Jesus' love. He broke every rule, yet kept the laws more devoutly than any before him. Such a contradiction frightened the priests.

As the disciples made ready to leave the upper room, my thoughts returned to what I saw before me. I could not understand the strange turn of events this evening.

Jesus told them he wished to go pray to his heavenly Father for strength to face the coming night. He chose the solitary, walled olive gardens known as Gethsemane, which overlooked the city. His choice came as no surprise. When the hordes of followers and worshipers had exhausted him, he would escape to this garden for rest, solitude, and fellowship with God. He favored the secluded olive grove with only one gate serving as both entrance and exit. At night, the gnarled olive trees cast shadows about the place, making it seem safe.

Although I knew of his love for that soothing retreat, my throat tightened as I realized how vulnerable he would be to attack there, hidden from the city, and the city hidden from him. Fear paralyzed me, and I stood rooted to the small prison formed by the screen hiding me from public view. I wanted to shout to Jesus not to leave the haven of Amashia's home. Despite my compelling urge to stop him, I could not move. Alas, my courage failed me, and I did not speak out when I had the opportunity. I, like the others with him, did nothing and said nothing.

When they finished the celebration, Jesus led a hymn with great enthusiasm. They went downstairs, and Jesus said to Amashia, "With your permission, we will leave now. We are going up to the Mount of Olives."

Amashia said, "Depart in peace." I thought this odd because normally she would accompany such an honored guest for a distance. She must have sensed the urgency in him to be about other business. She returned to her other guests and to me.

The unusual celebration ended with worry and tension thick in the air. The guests left and returned to their homes, and only Amashia and I remained. One of the servant boys spoke to me, asking, "Shall we clear the upper room? Do you wish to gather the food for the poor at the gate?" As if returning from a far away place, my attention focused on the familiar tasks awaiting me. My heart quickened, and I rushed to attend to these last duties of the evening. A terrible, unexplainable urgency filled my breast. Quickly, I completed the straightening of the upper room. Amashia came to the door. Her ample bosom heaved with the effort of climbing the stairs in haste. "Mary, what keeps you? The guests have all left the lower chamber, and your servants are waiting! I thought, perhaps, Judas was here saying farewell to you." Amashia spoke of Judas, as she looked about the upper room, searching the shadows. "Where is Judas? He did not leave with Jesus and the others."

"Jesus sent him on an errand early in the evening. He did not return," I replied. The words fell like stones from my lips. Some of Jesus' sadness invaded my heart, and I became apprehensive for my son. What could have kept him from the table on such an important night? Gazing through a window at the flickering lights of the city below the terrace, the penetrating darkness gave me no answers.

Amashia waved the two serving boys toward the kitchen and extinguished the few lamps still lighted. I carried one small lamp to light our way downstairs while Amashia chattered on about the large number of guests she had served in the lower rooms. My thoughts darted from one disciple to another as I tried to make sense of what had happened. I just could not understand what Jesus meant.

"Mary? Mary!" Amashia said. "You seem so distracted. I've been trying to get you to answer my question for some time now."

"I'm sorry. What did you say?" My mind could not focus on her news of old friends and distant relatives who had shared this holy meal. Repeatedly, I saw Judas's scowling countenance as he left the group.

"I asked how Judas seemed, but you are acting oddly. Now I'm beginning to wonder if something is wrong." Amashia's brows furrowed with worry.

"I am troubled by what I have witnessed tonight. I can't speak with you just now, Amashia."

Amashia nodded understandingly. With her arm around my shoulders, Amashia guided my lagging footsteps. "I enjoyed seeing my cousin Leye. She came tonight with her first son. They are just beginning their family. Our circle of family continues to grow larger every year. How Tahan would have enjoyed all these children in our home." I mused, *"We have been friends so long she feels my inner turmoil and is trying to lighten my mood with small talk."*

Just as we entered the great hall, Zilpah came to us. "The priests of the Temple called Simon away. He said you are to go home with your household, as he did not know what could have brought the priests' call. He asked you not to wait up for him. The household waits, and they are tired from the long day's labors." Zilpah finished her message, gently draped a soft robe around my shoulders, and pulled my veil across my face. Amashia accompanied us to the back garden. With a warm hug, she bade us a safe walk home. Zilpah's protective, gentle hand on my arm gave me comfort.

Once we reached our own garden gate, Zilpah hurriedly dispersed the servants to their quarters. She then led me to my chamber. Taking the robe from my shoulders, she bade me blessings of Passover and with tired steps disappeared through the darkness of the hall to her quarters. The house was eerily still. Even as I removed my clothing, I could not stop myself from listening intently. I knew not what sound my ears sought, but still I strained to hear.

The silence allowed me to ponder Simon's call to the Temple at such an unusual hour; yet I felt no fear for him. I suspected the priests wanted Simon's wisdom for some complicated question arising from the many pilgrims gathered there. My husband's kindness and fair judgments were so highly valued that the priests relied on him for many things. I comforted myself with the thought of his standing at the Temple.

Much time had gone by since that horrible ordeal started; yet, it was as fresh on my mind as if it were yesterday. I had experienced once more the feeling of anxiety and had retaken every step along the way to Amashia's house. As I relived the moment of Judas turning to me in his hour of distress, I could see he was not himself that fateful night. His haste to leave the upper room still haunts me. My body trembles with fear when I remember Judas's attempt to tell me what he had done. At no time is that memory far from my mind.

I had dreaded nights where I would lie listlessly upon my mat as sleep always came slowly. This night I turned, drew my body close beneath my cover, and slept fitfully through the night. I awakened in the morning feeling as though those two long days had never ended. I had repeatedly relived every detail. In anguish, I was determined to understand what I could have done to prevent all the tragedies of those two days.

Zilpah entered my chamber with a tray of tea and cakes. She said, "Mistress, have your tea and cakes while I lay out your dress for the day. I am taking you outside today. You have been in this room too long."

Ignoring her comments, I inquired, "Zilpah, How could I have missed the signs? What could I have done … ?"

Interrupting me, Zilpah firmly stated, "My lady, Stop asking such questions!" You are tormenting yourself. The entire household is feeling it. It had to be the way it was. Word has come to this house about Jesus' death being prophesied from long ago. As for Judas, we may never understand his motive, but I know he would not want you to continue to blame yourself. You must think of Simon now. You are both in such pain. You need each other. Forgive me, Mistress, for my forwardness. I am worried about you both."

Chapter 6

ilpah's words touched my soul, but how could I bridge the deep chasm existing between Simon and me? Our life together was almost intolerable. I could not bear to look at Simon or to speak to him, nor could he bear to look at me. We shared the same house but were unable to acknowledge each other. When I stole a glance at him, I could tell he had wrapped his shame and embarrassment around him like a cloak. His emotions seemed to immobilize his thinking, his actions, and his ability to feel. Although he went to the marketplace and conducted business with those who came to the city from afar, he left daily activities to his trusted servants. He chose to remain out of sight when people of Jerusalem came to his stall.

Simon no longer taught in the shadow of the inner court of the Temple. No urgent messages came summoning him to appear before the priests. In many ways, it was as if Simon had disappeared into the shallow grave of our disgraced son.

Shaking my head, I realized my grief, guilt, and shame had paralyzed my heart. Death dwelt inside my body, and I felt sure it had found a place inside Simon as well. No, not death! Death would have been a welcome relief from such grinding agony of the soul. The torture I felt for failing my husband and my son was much worse than anything death had to offer.

Simon's scornful eyes haunted me. I did not want to see him or anyone else. I went for days without eating or washing and had no thoughts for my household or myself. I wanted only to be alone to sift through the past. Searching for my failure as a mother, I lay in bed and lamented over Judas's childhood. What would I have done, if I had not had Zilpah? She was constantly concerned for me. She spoke with friends who came to call. Simon and I turned them away.

One day she said, "I fear for your life, Mary. You are wasting away. I fear you will die of the torment you heap upon yourself. Please, Amashia is here. You must see her today. She has come to see you many times, been refused and turned away. She says she will not leave the gate until you grant her an audience. She is your dearest friend Mary. She needs to see you, and you need to see her as well."

"Not today, Zilpah, I don't have the strength."

Listlessly, I turned my face to the wall, not even wishing to rise from my bed.

Lying in stillness, I heard the two women talking. I heard Zilpah tell Amashia, "I wish you could see Mary. Her once-beautiful eyes are now dull and glazed. She is without expression; the once ready smile seems gone forever."

Amashia sighed despairingly, "I don't know what to do. I am helpless to reach her. I know God does not will this for her."

"Amashia, the warmth and friendliness radiating from Mary have disappeared. She refuses to go anywhere or to see anyone. She believes she can never go out in public again. Her guilt is so deep she has cut herself off from her loved ones and all of her friends. I think she has distanced herself even from God. I am so afraid for her."

"I, too, fear for her, Zilpah. I am so grateful she has you to look after her. You are her only contact with those outside."

"I think of Mary before the betrayal. She had an enviable position within the city. Her once full life is now empty. You remember how she enjoyed the reputation of being a vital woman."

Zilpah paused and when she continued, her voice sounded strained, "I don't understand how all her wisdom and insight have deserted her. She sees her place of honor replaced with one of shame."

I listened without emotion. I felt they were discussing a stranger whom I did not know. I heard both women sobbing as I turned over and buried my head in my blanket. I covered my ears and never knew when Amashia left the hallway.

As the months went by, I took refuge in recalling Judas's childhood. Even though being a strong-willed child, he had delighted me from the day of his birth, bringing joy to the household. He always seemed to have a sweet in his hands, usually given to him by Zilpah. There never seemed to be enough delicacies in the household for him. He jealously guarded the baskets the servants filled for us, convinced they were for him alone.

As a young boy, not easily influenced by others, he often insisted other boys follow his ideas. Whenever the boys from the neighborhood played together, Judas provided the rules. If another boy argued with him over those rules, Judas provided reasoning to silence his dissent. Remembering his ability to get others to do things his way, I shook my head.

Judas had a knack for keeping himself fastidiously neat, never allowing a hair out of place or a mar on his clothing. He refused to allow himself to be soiled. Like his father, other people's opinions of him mattered. That is why Judas's decision to follow Jesus, a humble carpenter, surprised us all.

Repeatedly, I asked myself, where had I failed him? Could I be blind to the signs of his weakness? I only saw the strength he always radiated. I remember hearing about the time he got into an argument with one of the rabbis who taught him in the Temple school. I wish I knew about the part he played in the argument. Once, I remember Judas being sent home in a highly agitated state. He would not talk about what had happened. When Simon came home, I asked him about the incident. He waved his hand and dismissed it by telling me not to worry about men's business.

Judas always made me proud of his appearance, his scholarly abilities, and the way he took to his father's business. He seemed to have such a promising future in store for him; he held such promise. I had looked forward to a house full of grandchildren just like him.

When Judas reached an age to be married, he refused to marry Abigail, the woman I thought perfect for his bride. She came from a fine family and would have been the kind of wife to help him with his trade. She had many connections in the right places. She wanted to marry him, but Judas had no interest in her even though she was strikingly beautiful.

He loved a woman named Tamar, not a woman deserving of my son. She was so ordinary, with nothing to offer Judas. She lacked knowledge of the finer aspects of our culture. She came from an unknown family with no connections to help Judas. A common looking woman, she had nothing about her to draw people to her.

I never understood Judas's attraction to her, yet he enjoyed being around her. When I questioned him about her, he became angry. He would not discuss his feelings with me. He said over and over, "I know all the things she can't provide me, but that does not change how special she makes me feel. She looks up to me."

Neither Simon nor I approved of her, and as a result, Judas chose never to marry. At the time we were certain she looked toward Judas as a means of finding social prominence and money. I felt sad remembering he gave up what was very important to him in order to please us. I wondered if this had affected Judas more than I knew.

I wondered what else Judas had sacrificed in order to please others. Had he not been the strong-willed, self-reliant son I always imagined? Was there some part of Judas I had not known?

Upsetting myself became a daily ritual as I tried to discover why he betrayed Jesus and why he took his own life. I did not know this Judas. I could not forgive myself for the way we parted.

The only solace I found lay in my garden. I spent most of my days nurturing each little plant to grow. Only with my hands in the cool earth could I open my eyes to life or to beauty. During long hours there, I could escape from everyone, including the servants. I marveled at my ability to coax life from the earth. I felt assured my ability to produce any form of goodness had died with Judas. How ironic my garden flourished as my life faded!

I made it clear to Zilpah I would see no one. Yet, from time to time, she tried to persuade me when a close friend called at the gate. On one such day, I heard a voice from the life I had once lived.

"Mary, Naomi has stopped by to bring you greetings from all of the young wives you used to teach. She wants you to know they miss you and want you to return. They yearn for your help again. No one is better with fabric and a needle than you."

Zilpah's eyes pleaded with me to say yes. I did not want to disappoint Zilpah, but I continued to hesitate and make excuses.

"The time is not yet right. Go now, and offer her something to eat and drink. You may visit with her for a while."

Although I could not bring myself to face Naomi, I sat very still, wanting to hear every word of their conversation. Some part of me still longed to know what occurred outside my home. Naomi discussed with Zilpah how God continued pouring out his love and his gifts upon his followers.

"Zilpah, you must tell Mary of all the miracles taking place in the city. She needs to know the Lord is with us."

"Yes, she does need to know the Lord is still with us all," replied Zilpah.

Naomi rushed on, "Some of the people are receiving the

gift of prophecy. Those with this gift have insight into God's message and can foresee the needs of people. Some receive the gift of discernment. These people have the ability to know what is true or not true; what is coming from God or what is coming from man. Still others are growing in knowledge and wisdom."

"And how is this being received in the city?" inquired Zilpah.

Flushed with excitement, Naomi said, "Seeing the signs and wonders of God's power everywhere has lead to many new converts. The teachers are able to lay hands on people with afflictions, healing them immediately. Amazingly, some are even speaking in tongues foreign to them, and others who do not know the language can understand them. Miraculous things are happening among the followers of Jesus. Look at all the glorious things happening since his death." Naomi said, "Please tell Mary of these wondrous events. Tell her God has not left us, nor has he left her."

"I will tell Mary your good news, Naomi. Perhaps it will ease her pain if she can comprehend God is blessing his people with all these miracles."

Naomi got up to leave, then turning, she grabbed Zilpah's hand and said, "Mary must know, even with all the spiritual gifts God is pouring out, we have no one to instruct the wives and mothers on their role in God's New Kingdom. We desperately need her to return."

Zilpah replied simply, "I will deliver your message. Now, let me walk a short distance with you."

Watching the two women walk the stone path through the clump of trees to the main road, I contemplated all I overheard. *They still want me. How could they? Even Simon no longer acknowledges me. Such miracles are hard to imagine without seeing them. If only I am able to stay hidden from their sight, I want to observe what is happening.*

I began to think of my precious charges from what seemed like decades ago. My heart, numb for so long, melted as I thought of all the women I had taught through the years. I was so happy teaching the younger women not only how to mange their households, but also my greatest pleasure—the fine art of needle work. I felt privileged to teach the responsibilities of a wife passed down from generation to generation. That duty gave me great joy and pride, for I instructed them on the responsibilities I had learned from my mother, which she had in turn, learned from the mothers of long ago. Our traditions were long-standing, and we knew we were responsible for our husbands' happiness as well as for the development of our children's character. If we failed in our responsibility to them, we lost face and social acceptance; we ran the risk of our husbands casting us out.

Through the years, I had watched many women struggle with guilt when their children made wrong choices. Now it had become my struggle. I closed my eyes and saw the troubled faces of the women whose children caused them great grief. Ashamed, I recalled the self-righteous contempt I once felt for women whose children brought dishonor to their house. I sympathized with them now since I had developed a deeper understanding of their feelings.

What had become of the group of women I had abandoned in my shame? What had happened to them and their struggle with their children?

I thought of sweet and lovely Claudia. She and her daughter Leah shared a delicate and striking beauty. They had dark skin contrasted with bright green eyes. Even in veils, they

were distinguished from other women. All the women admired
Claudia's gentle and helpful demeanor. Any time one of the
women needed any kind of assistance, Claudia quietly stepped
in to help. Leah's personality, differing from her mother's out-
going nature, would almost fade away within any group. I had
never heard her state a desire to do anything by her own hand.
She depended upon Claudia constantly seeking her approval
and reassurance. Leah seemed to float through life with no will
of her own. If she had never done anything for herself, how
would she ever be able to do for her own household? Claudia
constantly worried Leah would never be confident enough to
marry and become mistress of her own home. How could such
a hesitant woman be responsible for the duties of motherhood?
What kind of husband would take her into his house? We could
depend on Claudia to question everything to get all the details.
Many of us feared Leah would live with her parents forever,
spiritless and dependent upon them for her every thought. I,
too, had been concerned about her daughter's apathy and felt
at a loss concerning how to guide her.

If Claudia was the deliberate and reserved woman of our
group, Naomi made up for it with her outspoken and impetuous
nature. She had a sixteen-year-old son named Eli. Unfortunately,
he had chosen boys who were known thieves and bullies as his
closest companions. As a result, Eli became notorious among
the young men who roamed the city. His preference for the old
city quarters, an area known for its brothels, distressed Naomi
the most. Poor Naomi! She constantly sought solace for the sorrow Eli heaped upon her.

Traditional Shisha was a comfort and a rock to her companions. She had observed every Holy day with a strictness nearing
the zealot's fervor. Her steadfast faith in God held fast no matter

what trials beset the chosen people. Her daughter Milcah rarely left her mother's sight. Milcah refused to consent to marriage with the young man chosen by her parents. Following this refusal, she quickly declared her intent to join the Essenes. She craved the simplicity of a life of denial of worldly comfort and eagerly sought the trials of poverty the Essene Sect offered. Her eyes glowed with zeal as she spoke of the purity of the people who lived in the wilderness. She often compared the young man who had introduced her to the Essenes' life to John the Baptist. My heart ached as I thought of the steadfast faith with which Shisha withstood Milcah's shocking decisions.

Alpheus's perpetually sulky expression popped into my mind. I remembered her frequently fussing over her only son, Nahor. Like a pomegranate, his nature had always been sour. Even as a child, he whined and ran to Alpheus when the other children did not do his bidding. Although a troublemaker and a bully as a young man, Alpheus continually blamed his problems upon his friends, the teachers at the Temple, the presence of the Romans, and anything else besides his temper. Despite Alpheus' consistent protection of Nahor from the consequences of his actions, he blamed her for his lack of success and his inability to form close friendships. He even blamed his mother for his irresponsibility.

Unlike Alpheus, Melita always exuded good humor. I smiled as I thought of her unruly brood never seemed to bother her. How she loved those active scamps! She had the most children of any of the young women in our group and wore that mantle with pride. Her children always seemed to be playing tricks on one another, tumbling about their mother's feet, and demanding dates and figs. I had never seen a mother work harder to give her children everything they wished. She anticipated their every need. Her house and gardens were always in a shamble. Her round lap was never empty, and the endless tugging on her braids never seemed to bother her. Their dirty hands and smiling faces were rewards cherished by Melita. She would always begin conversations at our meetings by relating the latest anecdote she had about her little pranksters. Her stories would make us laugh as we imagined all seven of her children running about and wreaking havoc. Surprising myself, I smiled at my memory of her. How long had it been since I smiled?

What a contrast Melita was to Damaris. Melita was short and portly, while Damaris stood tall and sturdy with a determined stride. Anyone seeing Damaris move about the markets immediately recognized her determination. Even the simplest decisions required cautious deliberation and confidence. I imagined her striding purposefully with her household servants, holding firmly to the hand of her son, Salah. She had directed him in every way as he grew from infancy to a young man. Even when Salah reached the age to accompany his father to the Temple for teaching, Damaris continued to give him stern direction. Unfortunately, his apparently docile nature cloaked his rebellion. He drowned his mother's control in strong wine. Often, his ne'er-do-well companions returned him in a state of unconsciousness to her gate, with his clothes soiled by drunken vomit and filth. He refused all urging to join his father in trade. His only ambition became oblivion through wine.

Then there was Sori, who took more responsibility for her mothering than the others because her husband was a trader traveling from city to city with his goods. The appearance of her frail frame did not convey her strength in caring for her sons as both mother and father. Sori's no-nonsense approach to life left her with problems expressing herself in public. I could never get her to respond to any discussion unless I asked her directly. When she did speak, we could rely on the truth of what she had to say. Her fair skin and fine hair contrasted her appearance different from the rest of us. Although slow to speak, Sori was quick to grasp the ideas and concepts we discussed and even quicker to put them into practice. She often dismissed the chitchat of the women as gossip and dawdling sometimes leaving her alienated from the group. Nevertheless, she never missed a meeting.

Recalling my memories of these women who had once held me in such high regard and respect, I cringed wondering what they must think of me now. As I pondered all my dear friends, who, like me, had tied their successes as mothers to the successes of their children, I could not shake the images of their familiar faces looking at me with blame. I could not bring myself to face them.

Chapter 7

For what seemed like an eternity, I refused to see any of my former friends. I could not bear to face them. The only beauty or solace in my life was my garden and its bounteous flowers. One day, as I entered the hall with my apron full of flowers, I heard Shisha talking with Zilpah. The sound of her voice brought a spark of life to my heart. Surprised, I thought, *"This is the first time I have felt any life in a long time."* I had become most fond of Shisha, one of the women Amashia and I had taught the rudiments of being a Jewish wife and mother. I wondered how she managed the daughter who distressed her so much. In my shame, I could not let her see me, so I kept quiet.

They did not know about my presence when I heard Shisha tell Zilpah, "The younger women have not gathered since the deaths of Jesus and Judas. Amashia feels she cannot lead the group alone—she is too devastated over Mary's heartbreak. Still, we have seen each other quite often, and we are meeting with the teachers of Jesus' message, trying to understand how his message applies to our daily lives. Please tell Mary how much we miss her and how we wish she would return to help us understand this new teaching."

Zilpah responded, "I will tell her, but I doubt she will listen. I cannot reach her anymore. She does not think anyone can see any good in her now. I have almost given up although I long to reach her heart. All of her friends have tried to let her know she is still loved and needed. You remember how she used to be—so warm and giving. Now, she moves slowly and remains expressionless. Mary looks years older and frequently does not reply when I call her name. I am very concerned about her."

"I am too," Shisha sighed. "We cannot forsake her. We must believe she will return to us. I must go now, but tell Mary I will return again." Zilpah walked a short distance with her as I slipped back to the garden. I did not wish her to know I had overheard their conversation.

Even as I began to turn the moist soil with my hands, Amashia's face rose before my eyes. She seemed to struggle to speak to me. The vision was so real I found myself reaching a soiled hand out to her. When I found only distance before me, I slumped to the earth and cried tears of loneliness.

Zilpah came into the garden with soft footsteps and knelt beside me. She placed a gentle hand on my head and brushed away a twig caught in my hair. Quietly she spoke to me, "Amashia has come and will not leave. She vows she will stay until you receive her. She is sitting in the midst of the kitchen with all the servants. You must allow her to sit with you a few moments."

Slowly, I raised my aching body and reached out to Zilpah. She led me to a nearby bench beneath an olive tree in full bloom. The beautiful, white blossoms had fallen to the ground, inviting peace. When I did not respond to Zilpah's request, she slipped away, returning quickly with a bowl of water to wash away the soil from my hands.

I closed my eyes and again Amashia's face rose before me. I could almost feel her sitting beside me. Suddenly, the familiar smell of cloves and honey, always lingering about Amashia, filled the air. My eyes quickly opened to behold dear Amashia's face just as I had seen it. The love emanating from her eyes warmed me and I could not resist touching her plump cheeks with my cold fingers. As I touched her face, Amashia reached up and clasped my thin hands in her soft palms. Without words, we both knew she had reached me in my dark prison of despair.

Hesitantly I whispered, "How do you spend your days?" Such a simple question, little did I know the answer would be the most complex I would ever hear. With the intensity and elation only she could find within her heart, Amashia began her miraculous revelation.

"As you know, Mary, my custom is to begin my day by spending time with God in morning prayers. My heart has been heavy for you for some time. On one particular morning, I prayed for your restoration. I have never prayed more earnestly. As I prepared to leave my quiet time with God, I heard a still voice within me speak, 'Amashia, I am well pleased with you. You have been a faithful servant and teacher, and now I have a special mission for you. You will be teaching mothers a great lesson, influencing women for generations to come.'"

Excitedly, Amashia continued with the message she had heard from God. "Amashia, you and Mary have given much to the welfare of many mothers and their children. As you continue to meet with me, I will guide you to bear even greater fruit."

"Amashia," I said, "This is more than I can understand. Are you telling me God spoke to you, a woman?"

"Oh, yes Mary! I heard his message clearly, though the voice was not audible. God even assured me he would use me to bring much good to you, my dear friend. Mary, God wants you to know how important you are to him. He knows the love you carry in your heart for him. He also knows you think he cannot love you because of Judas's act and his death. My precious friend, your guilt and shame have separated you from God, from me, and from all the people who love you, as well as from those whom you love. Mary, you withdrew, closed your heart, and allowed your remorse to come between all of us. Oh Mary, God is using your journey as a grieving mother to help all mothers, many of whom have taken on a false sense of responsibility for the choices of their children. God wants them to become free of unwarranted guilt and shame so they will be able to maintain a relationship with him and with their loved ones."

"We are to bring together the women we taught and to learn anew. Out of your painful experience, all of us will learn a great lesson about motherhood." Amashia went on, "Not quite believing what I heard, I questioned the Lord, 'I don't know how to do this. I do not understand what you are asking me to do. What can I teach women that will affect future generations?'"

"I was told not to be concerned. He will be the teacher and provide the message. I will only have to allow him to work through me. I said, 'Lord, I am willing. I do not know if I am able, but I am willing.'"

"His final words both comforted me and reassured me, 'Fear not, for I will be with you. My son died so all people will know my love for them. My grace has set my people free. Go, Amashia. You have great work to do.'"

I could tell from Amashia's excitement and exhilaration she truly believed God was planning to use her in a powerful way, a way she could not yet comprehend.

"I am awed at this assignment", Amashia continued. "God has already blessed me with gifts beyond my comprehension by bringing many women to learn from me. Now he is asking me to embark on something I have not done before. My spirit is filled with excitement, even though I have no idea where this will lead."

"There is joy in my heart as I anticipate a great awakening for women," she hurried on. "Remember when we were taught by Jesus, how we would sit around the table with him, and how he eagerly taught both women and men? Now, My Lord has given me a mission vital to all women of the world."

Astounded by the details of Amashia's news, I sat mesmerized. She was so enthusiastic that she did not realize how long she had spoken. Thinking how blessed she was with her assignment, I wanted to communicate my love for her and for her mission.

Hesitantly, I began to speak to her, "Amashia, you already have the trust of all the women because they see you as a wise woman of God. You listen so well that every woman feels important. They will be receptive to your teachings."

Amashia's face shone with light as she persisted, "When I first heard Jesus and his teachings, I immediately became intrigued with his message and became a faithful student. I gained peace and intimate communion with him. As you know Mary, I began to teach all of my household, friends, and neighbors who became followers. Jesus brought a message that has changed the way we live and think."

Somehow, hope broke through the darkness in my soul. I thought, *"This must be the beginning of new understandings. Amashia's message from God indicates some changes for women's hearts and minds."*

Amashia took me by the hand and said, "Mary, the women need you, and you need them. You must be present as we start this lesson God has to give us."

I dropped my head, and turned inward, suddenly fearful. *"No,"* I thought, *"I am not ready to face the women."*

"I am happy about your mission," I said after a long silence. "You can tell me more about it here in the garden."

Amashia searched my face as she reminded me, "As Jewish mothers, we have always been held accountable for our children's adult lives. If they are successful, it is our success. If they fail, it is our failure. If they sin, it is our sin. God is ready to teach us a new way of looking at motherhood and our responsibilities. You must join us. You may remain silent. You will not even have to lower your veil if you will just be with us. I will make it comfortable for you so you will be unrecognized until you are ready to participate. There will be no more discussion about this."

With that statement, we sat side by side, lost in our thoughts about the mission from God. My thoughts turned to the way we as Hebrew women, viewed our role as mothers. Tradition dictated we willingly accept full responsibility for our children's successes and failures.

Eventually Amashia stirred and said, "I need to send word to the other women we will meet in the Women's Court at the Temple on the fourth day. Be prepared to be there, Mary. I will come by for you so you will not go alone." She rose, embraced me, and looking deeply into my eyes, said, "We must prepare for our new work. I will take my leave now."

I walked with her without speaking until we reached Zilpah. I asked, "Zilpah, Please walk part way with Amashia. Keep my friend company." We embraced and Zilpah saw her off by accompanying her for some distance.

After Amashia left me, I returned to the garden and sat in pensive reverie. The last year of my life seemed to flow through the river of my memory. I could see myself wandering the halls without awareness of the beauty surrounding me. The servants whispered in my presence as if they might awaken me from a deep sleep, closing doors softly. Locked gates kept the outside world at a distance. Zilpah placed a small drape over my window to mute the light entering my chamber. She placed food before me, yet I only wanted to have it removed. No delicacy enticed me, and no aroma tempted my appetite.

I had essentially disappeared from my own home. Simon was not a part of the flow of scenes passing through my mind. Where had he been while I hid within a haze of pain and shame? What had he done to heal the rent in his heart left by Judas's betrayal and death? When had we begun to avoid passing each other in our daily lives within our own home? These questions came as a shock to me.

Although Simon had denounced me to all when he saw Judas's body, his grief was certainly no less than mine. The loss of his only son must have left as deep a wound in his heart as it had in mine. Surely, at some time, I had gone to him to share his grief and his pain. Yet, even as that thought crept into my mind, I knew I had not. The shame of having mothered a son who brought disgrace to his father had locked me into a cell more solid than the ancient burial catacombs beneath the city. Simon and I both existed in a wasteland of terrible disgrace nourished by unspoken mutual denial. I had failed to go to Simon and offer comfort just as he had failed to come to me to offer private retraction of his public rejection of me. We had both failed each other in our greatest hour of need. The sins of pride, self-pity, and shame had replaced our once warm feelings for each other.

Shadows were lengthening as I arose from the garden bench and made my way into the kitchen. While preparing the evening meal, Zilpah bustled about and managed her young sons by keeping them busy and out of mischief. Heat from the ovens just outside the door wafted through the open windows, bearing the aroma of baking bread. Spices hung from the walls, filling the room with pungent odors. For the first time in a long time, my senses were returning and I began to feel the desire for food.

All eyes were on the tasks at hand; yet I felt them watching me, waiting to see if I would wander through like a ghost or if I would stop and take up my role as wife of the house. I was not yet ready to tackle that task. Still, with a smile of true gratitude for their kindness and devotion through my dark ordeal, I handed each one a flower I had brought in from the garden.

As I made my way to my room where I would receive the evening meal, Simon entered the corridor. For the first time since Judas's death, I interrupted our silence by murmuring to Simon, "Amashia visited me today. She brought you figs." Startled by my words, he stopped, and then looking straight ahead, he grunted something indistinguishable. We exchanged nothing else between us; yet, I felt relieved the silence had been broken.

That night I fell into a deep sleep. Although I still dreaded the thought of leaving the seclusion and safety of Simon's house, I knew Amashia would not accept my reluctance to face the women. As I slept, I had a dream so vivid it seemed real. I walked among women whom I had seen many times. They looked at me with their faces hidden behind veils; each one was wearing their finest garments. Their feet were shod in sandals of burnished fabrics from exotic lands. Retracing my steps, I saw their eyes were all downcast. As I reached out to touch them and bring their gaze to mine, each one I touched dropped her veil, and I saw an unfamiliar face revealed. None of them smiled, but some retained a peaceful gaze while other eyes filled with sorrow and pain. The sun rested on those who had peace, but seemed dim over the ones in sorrow. I felt great sympathy for all the women. Somehow, they seemed to be waiting for me to do something for them or to give something to them. I kept walking among them, touching them, and looking into those beseeching eyes. When I awoke, the dream would not leave me.

I lay back and pondered the mystery of the dream. If only I could wake Simon, he could tell me the meaning. I knew the moment I had the thought, God sent this dream to me, and only I could find the answer to my questions. One way or another, this dream had intertwined itself with Amashia's vision.

Chapter 8

My body would not rest on the mat. I tossed and turned while I wrestled with the problem of joining Amashia in the morning. How could I face all the women? I had dwelt only with the demons of guilt and shame since Judas's death. Yet, I desperately wanted the blessing of Amashia's message. How I dreaded the moment when those who had formerly admired and envied me as a wife and mother, would now look upon me in judgment. My sleeping mat became a place of torment as I lay awake hour after hour, recalling my son's behavior leading to Jesus' death and my husband's harsh public denial of me. Once again, I envisioned the eyes of public judgment—accusing eyes mocking and focused on me—the ultimate failure as a mother. Finally, just before dawn, I determined I would rather face the women I had known and taught so long ago than to go through one more day of this torment. I would go to the Temple and listen as Amashia taught, but I would remain veiled and hidden from the others. My confidence, riddled with guilt and shame, created doubt as to whether I could withstand the stares I imagined coming from those recognizing me as Judas's mother. Amashia would have to bear the burden alone of teaching these young women. My very presence would be an offense to them. How sorrowful I felt for the shame and disgrace I carried wherever I went. Still, Amashia's message was surely worth venturing beyond my gates.

Having finally made my decision, I fell into a restful sleep. When the first sliver of light shone through my chamber window, I realized Zilpah had removed the drape she had put there. For the first time in many months, the rosy hue of dawn became visible to me. As I gazed at the faint light, my unease returned. Still, some glimmer of hope held me fast to my decision to hear Amashia's teaching just this once.

As if still in a strange dream, I prepared myself to go with Amashia to the Temple. When Zilpah came into my chamber, she made no comment about my being dressed for the streets. Instead, she came to me and gently rearranged my girdle to make my garment fit my delicate frame.

Satisfied, she gave me a pat of encouragement and a warm smile. "I saw Amashia and her servants coming through the kitchen garden. She will be waiting for you to go to the Temple. You'd best go directly to her."

With this brief message, Zilpah turned and briskly walked into the hall. I followed her and soon heard Amashia's hearty laughter filling the kitchen. She always found a kind word for each of the servants and often brought some special delicacy to the young children from her magnificent orchard and garden. Her husband had been curious about foreign plants, always coming home from his travels with new varieties of rare fruits and nuts. She generously shared these treasures from her garden.

"Ah, Mary, you come at just the right time. I have no more treats and soon I shall be reduced to picking figs from your trees for these hungry children."

Shaking her head in mock admonishment at the smiling children, she folded me in her warm embrace and turned me toward the door. As if she were taking up a discussion only briefly interrupted, she chattered on, "I think it best we take the back ways until we are outside the upper level. So many strange travelers are in the city and they bring such smelly goods! One's nose can barely survive the odors of the markets, much less all those straggling gentiles. One of my overseers told me he saw strange furs all the way from faraway barbarian cold countries. The furs are dark and heavy with huge clawed paws left on them. It's enough to give you strange visions just thinking about it!"

My throat almost choked with tears of thankfulness to dear Amashia. She had made an excuse to avoid the prying eyes of those who would recognize me. Once outside our own upper level community, I would be just another veiled woman walking toward the markets with household servants accompanying me. No one would recognize me as Judas's mother. Only when we entered the women's presence at the courtyard would I have to endure stares and unuttered rebukes. Fearing these women would sit in judgment of me, because I had failed to meet the measure of tradition, I remained well hidden.

Dread seeped into every pore of my skin. I felt smothered by my outer robes and my concealing veil as I neared the Temple. My feet seemed leaden and reluctant to move forward at the pace Amashia set. Sensing my hesitation, Amashia grasped my hand and held it tightly. The warmth and love she sent through that touch gave me courage and I forced myself to move forward again. Nonetheless, I could not raise my eyes from the dusty ground of the courtyard and surely would have stumbled without her strong grasp.

Once we reached the Women's Court, Amashia motioned to a group of young wives who were already sitting beneath a portico. We entered without conversation. Amashia's handmaidens surrounded me and I went past the waving group unnoticed. The broiling sun created golden clouds from the whorls of dust kicked up by the women's trailing robes on the well-trodden pathways. Even the olive trees looked dusty and sparse in this part of the courtyard. Quickly, I took my place behind a huge column hiding me from the other women, yet allowing me to see and hear Amashia clearly. I tugged my veil even higher so only the barest slit allowed my eyes vision.

I distracted myself from my apprehension by watching Amashia and one of her household maidens lay out trays of sweet dates and figs alongside small breads sprinkled with toasted seeds. A large basket of grapes finished the preparation of food she had for the young wives. I could not help but admire the artistry Amashia used to arrange the fruits on the trays and the elaborate embroidery on the towels covering them. By Amashia's lovely example, a wife complements her husband's wisdom in choosing her by paying attention to clever details.

Surely, the women would see the importance of attention to the smallest detail in making each meal a celebration of love in her home.

What a beautiful sight Amashia was that fateful day! She removed her outer garment of dark blue revealing a rich purple tunic with voluminous sleeves flowing about as she moved her arms. The richly embroidered girdle with pale purple flowers bound around her sturdy waist matched the sandals on her feet, intertwining the same embroidered ties. Sun glinted off her shining dark hair, giving the impression of glittering jewels hidden in the heavy braids.

Taking her place before the women, Amashia stood to her fullest height and raised her arms to heaven praying—her face a visage of rapture. Silence descended upon the group of talking women. I looked about, for these were women I loved and for whom I had spent many hours instructing in the traditions expected of a wife and mother. Remembering each one, and the struggles they faced as mothers, I knew they thirsted for Amashia's message just as lost travelers in the desert thirst for the sight of water.

"My sisters," Amashia said bowing slightly, "My mind, my voice, and my heart are here to serve each of you. As you know, wonderful things have been happening to those of us who are followers of the Nazarene. God has given men and women alike so many gifts of understanding and knowledge. Out of my deep desire to help our friend Mary, I beseeched the Holy Spirit to intercede on her behalf. I prayed for a sign, an omen. God has spoken to me not only about Mary, but also about all women."

Disbelieving what she heard, Shisha interrupted asking, "Amashia, do you mean God spoke to you, a woman?"

"Yes, Shisha, I have heard from God. The voice was not audible, yet, I know the message did not come from my own mind. I am confident the words came from God, because they have never been my thoughts. In fact, the message was contrary to my own beliefs. Yet they follow the principles the Master taught us. When I first heard from God, I was as surprised as you are. We must all remember God has been doing many miraculous things since Pentecost. Many of our brothers and sisters are hearing from God."

"I am eager to tell you about a mission God has given us. As you well know, our traditions of old taught us to take full responsibility for the successes, for the failures, and for the choices of our children. Our worth as mothers depends on how well our children serve in the family, the community, and the Temple. This proved to be a heavy burden for us to bear. We bore full responsibility without holding our children accountable for their actions. We acted as if we were their only influence." Moaning and groaning came from the women acknowledging the truth of Amashia's statement.

"God wants us to understand the difference between false responsibility and our true responsibility. We are to learn how to raise children who assume responsibility for their actions or inactions. He has selected me, the unlikeliest of women, to bring you his message by putting the lessons in my heart so I can instruct you on how to use this new understanding in your lives."

Once again, Shisha stood saying, "Amashia, this frightens me—hearing from God and telling us new ways to raise our children."

"Shisha, I understand your fear. Once you hear the teachings, you will see there is nothing to fear. You can be assured it is in harmony with what the Master taught, and what the prophets of old taught. Each of us will be the only one held accountable for our own life when it is over. Can we all agree to wait until we hear the messages before drawing conclusions?"

"That is why we try to protect them," Naomi said almost in tears. "We know they will be held accountable."

"Yes, Naomi, and this is why the message God has for us is so very important. I hear your fear. Would you be willing to learn what he has for us before you decide its validity?"

With some hesitation, the women slowly nodded their heads in acknowledgment.

"With your permission, I would like to tell you more about the message I heard from the Lord. We can all agree the way we have always interpreted responsibility has caused us much pain. Sometimes it has led us to experience much guilt." Faint murmurings came from the women. Amashia quieted the women and continued, "Our Lord wants us to have a clear understanding of our responsibility as mothers so we can raise responsible children. Today's teaching will help free us from the burden of guilt we carry, coming from false responsibility."

Obviously distressed, Claudia asked, " Our guilt comes from false responsibility? How can that be?" "What is false responsibility? I have never heard of such a thing."

"Let us look to God as our example to understand your questions and this lesson. Remember God's first children, Adam and Eve. He gave them a beautiful garden for a home, and all they could need or want. They were close companions as he walked and talked with them each evening. No one has been closer to him than Adam and Eve, except his son Jesus. God denied them only one thing; they were not to eat of the tree of knowledge of good and evil, for if they did, they would surely die. They chose to do the very thing he had forbidden. Here is where we learn our lesson.

"Adam and Eve's failure was not God's failure; he had instructed them well. Their disobedience was their own failure, as it is when we have instructed our children well and they are disobedient. God gave his children choice and they experienced the consequences of those choices. False responsibility is taking responsibility for people and things we have no right or power to control."

I caught my breath when I heard what Amashia said, shocked at the obvious truth. Glancing at the other women, the awe I saw in their faces reflected my feelings.

After allowing time for reflection, Amashia continued with other examples to deepen her message. "God delivered our ancestors out of slavery and bondage from the Egyptians. They fled with Moses, and God made it possible for them to cross the Red Sea on dry land. Even though they experienced God's deliverance and miracles, they lost faith quickly and built a golden calf to worship. Did God fail them? No! Just the opposite happened. They failed God and themselves."

Because he only desires good for his children, "God gave the Ten Commandments to his sons and daughters so they could live in love and harmony with him and with one another. Those commandments are a pathway to right behavior leading to true peace and happiness. Yet, few people have kept all his commandments. When we teach our children God's ways, their failures are not our failures any more than when God taught his children, and they were disobedient. Look to God as your example instead of looking to tradition."

Finished with her message, Amashia sat in stillness and

gazed into the eyes of each woman as if waiting for a response. The profound silence permeated the crowd. I sat in wonder at what I had heard.

Shaking her head, Esther broke the quite by saying, "When my child or Claudia's child makes a mistake, we have been taught it's our fault. Our mothers raised us this way, and our grandmothers raised them that way. This is unthinkable."

Shisha spoke up grudgingly, "I admit I've been feeling guilty because Milcah is so head-strong. She refuses her arranged marriage and is determined to pursue a life in the Essene Sect."

"Shisha, where do you think you failed in your responsibility?" questioned Amashia.

"I don't know, but I must have." Shisha stood fast in her belief.

Damaris added, "If we do things correctly and teach our children correctly, we believe our children will make good decisions."

"Yes, Damaris, and many times they do," responded Amashia. "However, sometimes they don't regardless of how right the teaching. I think your belief is a common conviction too often making too many of us feel like failures and thus feel guilty. Let us further explore this insight. Remember, God is our example. Adam and Eve ate the fruit of the forbidden tree. They were tempted and they listened to the tempter, not to God. Look at our logic in light of this information. If we continue to believe we have failed after we have taught our children well, then we must believe God failed Adam and Eve because they made a wrong decision."

Gasping, Shisha blurted, "But we are not God! We would never think of God doing anything wrong. He is infallible!"

"If we apply the reasoning we use on our self to his relationship with his creation, we have to say, he did fail," said Amashia.

It is not about God's failing or succeeding. God taught. People chose. It's about everyone having choice, and God is not responsible for his children's choices. Nor, are you!"

I had taught other women. Could I be hearing right? This reasoning was contrary to our beliefs. My heart pounded with both fear and hope.

Amashia continued, "Our challenge is to recognize when our responsibility ends, and when our children's begins."

After an endless silence, Damaris spoke hesitatingly, "Amashia, what a revelation! I need time to consider all I have heard. What we have believed for generations suddenly is changing."

"Yes, that is true," said Amashia. "God wants to lighten our burden by pointing out the error of our beliefs. False responsibility causes us to feel guilty. When we feel guilty, we have a tendency to overindulge our children. In addition, guilt leads to feelings of unworthiness. Unworthiness causes us to withdraw from our relationship with God."

That is exactly what I have done, except I have not only withdrawn from God, but also from everyone and everything holding significance in my life. This thought alarmed me.

After another long pause, Naomi spoke up. "I can tell you I feel unworthy, I feel guilty, and I feel shame. My son Eli is captivated with the harlots in town, and he makes no secret of it. There are so many harlots now, and when he is not visiting them, he seems to be thinking about them. I feel I have failed as a mother because he is so intrigued with them, and there is nothing I can do or say to keep him away from those awful women."

"Naomi, have you taught Eli about God's wishes concerning his children and their sexual activity?" Amashia asked calmly.

"Yes, I have, many times." Naomi bristled.

"Naomi, I know you have also talked to him about what might happen to him physically as a result of these visits," Amashia gently nudged.

"Yes, I have. I have told him those whores are carriers of unspeakable diseases. I have done everything I know to do without tying him to his own bed." Naomi began to wring her hands. Obviously humiliated, she dropped her head as though to become invisible.

"Naomi has done all she can, Amashia!" Shisha jumped to Naomi's defense.

Studying Naomi's eyes, Amashia said to her, "Naomi, you have taught him what God wants, what being a man entails, and what consequences his sexual behavior may have. You have also been an example to him by being Godly and practicing fidelity. You have done all you can. This is what God is telling you today. Eli is no longer your responsibility. The failure is his, not yours. This is now between Eli and God."

"I don't understand. It is all so frustrating," Naomi wailed.

"Naomi, what proof do you have that leads you to believe you are a failure as Eli's mother?"

Turning to the other women, Amashia said, "We must look at what our tradition has taught us. Where did our belief in our failure come from? How did each of us come to fear failing our children?"

Ignoring the questions, Shisha retorted, "We all feel the same way. We are all frustrated." With blank faces, the women looked at each other and then at Amashia.

Amashia continued, "We are being unreasonable. We insist on arguing for tradition, and we argue against what God wants us to understand. My dear sisters, we must consider all the times God's children disobeyed him and made destructive choices. Do we think we can do better than God does—never have our children be disobedient and make wrong choices? How arrogant of us!"

Amashia's pointed question provided us with a different perspective than we had considered. Although hesitant, Naomi finally said, "Let me try to understand this. I taught Eli the right ways. Are you telling me Eli has chosen the wrong way, and I am not at fault?" Not waiting for an answer, she continued, "How can this be? I thought I should have the ability to prevent Eli from becoming involved with the women who fascinate him. Yet, no matter what I say or do, he is still determined to seek out harlots. According to you Amashia, God is telling me his choices are not my failure."

Amashia's face beamed with the comprehension taking place. She said, "This is what each of us needs to understand. We, as mothers, have limitations in what we can do. You have taught him right from wrong. God has given everyone free will. Eli has chosen waywardness at this time."

Naomi responded, "But I still feel so guilty!"

"Are you going to argue for your feelings, Naomi, or accept the freedom God is offering you?" Amashia declared.

Sori sat quietly among the women never saying a word, but from the intensity on her face, she had not missed anything. This had been her pattern in our previous meetings.

The women buzzed among themselves as they tried to determine the meaning of this freeing thought. I felt as lost as they looked. Wayward sons were such shameful reflections on their mothers. Naomi's habitual complaining had often been irritating to me, but now I felt a kinship with her I had not known before.

"My sisters, this has been a lot for us to absorb today," said

Amashia. "We need to pray and think about what we have heard until it penetrates our thinking and releases us from false responsibility."

"I chose for us to meet on this day when the moon is new, representing new beginnings for us. Let us come back together at the next new moon and continue unraveling God's message. My prayers will be with all of you. Each day I will pray for God to help us gain the wisdom and understanding he has for all mothers."

She waved her arms toward the plentiful trays of food awaiting the women. "Come and share this food so we may gain strength in our bodies for our journey home. God has fed our souls. Now we shall feed our bodies and share our friendship."

Amashia's handmaidens had come to sit around me and protect me from any searching eyes, so I remained well out of sight where no one would note my presence. Carefully, I drew even farther behind the column and did not move, lest I draw attention to myself. My breath seemed trapped in my breast and my mind became fraught with confusion at Amashia's words. I needed to sort out all I heard. I needed to get away. Amashia must have sensed my discomfort. She slipped away from the others to speak to me.

"I am glad you are here beside me, my dear Mary. I know you have much to think about, and you must be tired on this, your first day away from your house. Zeb and one of my handmaidens will walk you home. I cannot leave now because so many here have questions. Rather than liberation, some seem to feel distressed. We will come together next week to study further God's will for us." She hurriedly embraced me and I slipped away unnoticed as the women shared the food Amashia had prepared for them.

My mind whirled with the new teaching I had heard. I knew I must tell Simon something of this turn of events. Yet, how could I tell him our beliefs about the false responsibilities of a mother were not the true will of God? Although in turmoil because of Simon's possible rejection, I wanted and needed to tell him. I hurried along in silence behind Zeb.

Zeb chose the crowded streets for our route home. My mind swelled and swirled with Amashia's message. I took no notice of the crowd trudging through the dusty streets. As the familiar walls of home loomed before me, I was startled. For the first time in more than a year, I had put aside my personal grief and shame. I did not know whether eyes had stared in disgust or in sympathy, and even more surprising to me, for a brief time I felt no need to hide from others. The wonder of Amashia's revelations had totally engrossed my thoughts.

I gazed at the high wall of simple rough rocks and mortar surrounding our home. The tops of the trees in the small cedar grove inside the walls hid the house from view. How fresh and inviting those cool, dark cedars looked to me after my exhausting day among the crowds. My heart stirred with a gladness to be near the haven of home. I knew this was where I belonged. This was where God had placed me, and I felt deep thankfulness to return.

Zeb rapped on the small gate, and it quickly opened. We entered and he exchanged greetings with the elderly gatekeeper. I hurried on toward the house of Simon, shining with invitation in the bright sunlight.

As I neared the open door, I saw Zilpah waiting with a tender smile of welcome. She tended my veil and outer garment. Another servant tended to the washing of my dusty feet.

I washed my perspiring face and neck with cool towels. Zilpah kept silent, but I knew she was eager to know about my first endeavor outside the walls of home.

"Come, Zilpah, let us go to the kitchen and I will tell you what I learned today."

Zilpah busied herself with making tea. When the tea was ready, she settled in, ready to listen. Her eyes fastened on me as I began, "I am still feeling stunned by what I heard today. God wants mothers to let go of their false responsibility and focus on our true responsibility."

"False responsibility," questioned Zilpah, "what is false about being responsible?"

"It's hard to understand, isn't it?" I said, taking the tea she held out to me. "This new message is quite different from what we have always believed. As you know, we women have always accepted responsibility for everything our children do and do not do. We even feel responsible for our husband's happiness or unhappiness. Accepting there are things for which we cannot be responsible is going to take time."

Interrupting, Zilpah asked, "Are you sure this message is from God?"

"Zilpah, Amashia said we must discern the difference between true responsibility and false responsibility by looking to God as our example. In the scriptures of old, we are referred to as God's children. God is our spiritual parent. He taught his children well, and still they are too often disobedient. God reminded us he taught Adam and Eve yet, they disobeyed him. He brought our ancestors out of bondage and then they made a golden calf to worship. Zilpah, he gave us his ten commandments to live by and still his people break his laws."

Zilpah interjected, "It's easy to understand God is not responsible for his children's disobedience. It's not so easy for me to draw the same conclusion about myself or other mothers."

"No, it's not easy, I still feel responsible for Judas's actions. I am not sure I will ever get over that."

"Please rest Mary. I must prepare the evening meal. Simon will be returning soon."

I realized Zilpah was right. I had not noticed the tiredness in my body. This outing was my first exertion of any kind since Judas's death. As I continued to ponder the possibility of false responsibility, I went into my room and lay down on my mat. Within moments, I fell asleep.

The aroma of cooking drifted from the kitchen, slowly reviving me. For the first time, in a long time, I had an appetite. The scent of bread fresh from the oven was absolutely tantalizing, and I resolved tonight I would sit down to a meal. I would not have food brought to my room any longer. The thought of being around my household was pleasant.

Frightened to tell Simon, I rejoined the small group of women, my imagination raced through possible conversations and responses. Perhaps he would be as amazed as I had been God had spoken to Amashia. On the other hand, Simon might reject the very idea God would speak to a mere woman. After months of avoiding each other, he might simply continue to ignore me. Perhaps he would be angry or disgusted. I thought of words that might open discussion with my husband whose distance from me was seemingly impenetrable.

Cautiously, I made my way down the hall to Simon's room. I lifted my hand and knocked on the door. Receiving no answer, I endured several moments of panic. Finally, I collected myself and timidly pushed the door open. Simon looked up dispiritedly from where he lay on his mat and raised himself on one elbow, the only acknowledgment he gave of my presence. My throat tightened to the point of choking. The many eloquent words I practiced in my mind escaped me. Wringing my hands with fear, I stepped forward until I stood before him. Taking a deep breath, I blurted out my news.

"Simon, I went to the Women's Court today. It's only the second time I have left your house since Judas's death. I left because of Amashia's revelation for mothers now and in the time to come. Surely, God has chosen her because of her pure heart and her love for his son, Jesus. She speaks with an authority, clearly emanating from the Father."

Having waited for a response and receiving none, I quietly muttered, "We will continue to meet together."

After some time, Simon spoke in serious tones, "Mary, you are the one who must pray about joining these women in the Temple court. I cannot give you an answer because I have no answers, not even for myself. I do know you cannot continue to hide behind these walls for the rest of your life."

My heart ached to hear more. Simon merely slumped back on his mat. He gazed at me for a moment longer with what I imagined contempt, then sighing he turned his face to the wall.

Discharged in this way, I fled back to the safety of the corridor. Relief flooded me as I realized Simon left the decision to me whether to continue on this journey.

Zilpah and I looked at each other questioningly from time to time, but we did not bring up the subject of the new revelation again. Amashia came by two days before our next meeting. I heard her exuberant voice all the way from the gated entrance as she greeted Zilpah. I walked to the entrance, inviting her to join me in the garden. Amashia's hardy embrace felt comforting and dispelled much of my inner unrest. I had hoped to discuss my turmoil with her before our next meeting.

We both started for the garden without saying a word. When we reached our favorite spot where we often went for good conversation, Amashia asked, "Mary, have you thought about what we learned from God?"

"Yes, that is all I can think about and I am quite troubled, Amashia. This idea of false responsibility is hard for me to accept. My mind refuses to retain it. It flies in the face of tradition. Perhaps future lessons will help all of us to gain better understanding of what God wants us to know about motherhood."

Chapter 9

Preparations for accompanying Amashia to the Temple were few since I cared little about my appearance. The tunic I wore looked old and worn as it hung loosely on my now frail body. With no thought for the vanities of beauty or impressing others, I chose an old black outer robe, one I often wore to the market when rain fell. Wrapping the well-worn garment around my shoulders, I walked through the hall into the kitchen.

"Zilpah, I am leaving now to go with Amashia to the Temple once again." Without hesitating, I made my way to the back gate to await Amashia's arrival. I gazed about the kitchen garden and orchard, trying to remember when we planted each fruit or vegetable. The mixture of spices growing near the gate gave a pungent, wild aroma to the morning air. My mind darted about like a firefly, trying to avoid the message Amashia planned to deliver today. Hearing her footsteps approach, I could evade it no longer.

Amashia swung the gate wide and swept inside. Abruptly, she stopped her swift steps and greeted me. "Ah, Mary! You are ready to go! This is good because we have brought special delicacies for our young women and need more time to make ready for them." With this comment, she grasped my arm and led me out of the garden. I heard the sturdy shaft of wood slide into the lock on the gate, and I shuddered at the sound. There was no turning back now.

Uncomfortable and nervous, a wave of nausea swept over me. *Maybe I am not ready for Amashia's message.* Maybe I should not go today. I realized with a start that I did not wish to avoid Amashia's insights. I wished to avoid the judgment and blame of the other women. I feared the women would judge me harshly if they knew who hid behind the full veil.

Again, we trudged through the crowds that were teeming in the market and outside the Temple where many pilgrims bargained with the gentile shopkeepers for sacrificial doves and first-born lambs. Jewish law makes it difficult to trade with the defiled gentiles to obtain animals to offer in sacrifice. Forbidden to touch their garments, we kept at distance. Even so, necessity compelled us to trade with the gentiles, and we managed to obtain the animals without defiling ourselves. The clever gentiles handled the sheep and oxen only with rods, with no touch of their hands. Thus, they presented the animals without coming

too near us devout Jews. Buyers placed their money in a copper
bowl just within reach of the crook of a shepherd's rod. The
trade completed, the gentiles deftly retrieved the bowl and pock-
eted the money within the folds of ragged garments.

The cries of the gentiles who provided the sacrificial animals
were always loud and plaintive. "Buy from me! I am so poor I
cannot feed my hungry children! My prices are the lowest in the
city! Alas, we shall starve if I continue to ask so little for such fine
animals!" I had never really listened to or looked at the scene
before. It was so commonplace my eyes had taken much for
granted, but my mind had not paid attention. Clearly, I could
see the mockery of the entire process. Why had I not seen it
before today? Were there other things I had ignored throughout
the years? Was I the only Jew who saw the elaborate behaviors of
the pilgrims as a game where each side pretended to be blind
to the other's actual part? Obviously, the gentiles had touched
the animals many times from their birthing to their offering at
the Temple. Yet, everyone acted as if this were not so. My mind
whirled, wondering how many other things we ignored by pre-
tending everything was as it should be.

Our early arrival allowed me to help Amashia and her handmaidens set out the food they carried. We were almost finished
when I heard Alpheus's strident voice complaining yet again
that her son became the victim of unfair treatment. I quickly
stepped behind the great column and settled myself in its shadow. I yearned to be near Amashia as she delivered her message.
Yet, the fear of all the women pointing to me and judging my
failure brought tears of frustration and shame to my eyes.

Amashia's joyful voice called me back from the darkness of
sorrowful memory. I roused myself and gazed at her glowing
countenance. God had truly touched her. She glowed with a

light shining all around her. I could not take my eyes from her as she spoke.

Amashia raised her arms to bring the women to attention. All the high-pitched voices quieted. Every woman sat gazing at Amashia expectantly. "Welcome my sisters. I am excited to see you back with us today. You had much to think about since our last meeting. The moon has made a full circle since we last met. You have had time to think prayerfully about the new concepts. Now let us discuss what you have been mulling over in your mind since our first meeting."

"I have always been taught I am responsible for how my child turned out," Rebecca said. "I have found myself both hopeful and confused to even consider I am not always responsible for my children's happiness and their success in life."

I watched all the women nod in agreement. Damaris spoke. "Since our last meeting, I have been making an allowance for the possibility I am not responsible for Salah's drinking. He frequents the old city with a rowdy group of young men, all from better families. They are only interested in having a good time. Their idea of fun is to get drunk and stay that way. They get into all manners of mischief; fighting and even destroying property. I feel so ashamed for letting this happen to him. I could control him as a child, but I cannot control him now. Salah did nothing wrong when little. He was perfect. I made sure of that."

Amashia said, "Damaris, you made an important point. You could control Salah when young, but you can't now." She continued, "How many of you recognize your need to control your children?" Several hands went up and still other heads nodded.

Amashia continued, "The lesson God has put in my heart

for today is about control." All eyes turned to Amashia as a holy presence seemed to surround her. Compassion showed in her soft face and filled her eyes as words flowed forth. "Today's lesson will free us and our children from the consequences of false responsibility. When we feel responsible for what we cannot control, we feel guilty. So let us explore control. When we feel responsible for the successes and failures of our children, we try to control our children's thinking, their actions, their emotions and their deeds. Wanting to protect our children is a natural instinct. In our attempt to protect them, we resort to control."

The women became restless, shifting about as they looked at each other with questioning eyes. Melita spoke, "Of course we are to control our children, how else we can protect them?"

Amashia continued, "When we believe our children's failures are our failures; we try to control them so we will not fail and avoid guilt. Our need to control comes from our fear our children cannot make right decisions without our telling them what to do. To change the way we are raising our children, it is necessary to understand how control affects the child. Our controlling nature leaves our children with no trust in their own abilities. When our babes develop the ability to understand our teachings for themselves, we must then turn loose of control. Control squelches God's spirit in them. None of us would ever want to do that! Not only do we squelch God's spirit in them, we also stifle their own spirit keeping them from developing their individual talents and fulfilling God's purpose for their life."

The women gasped at such a thought, as did I along with them.

Amashia determined we would fully grasp the message said, "Here is what we have to understand. Control defeats our intention to be protective and results in the child doubting her own capabilities. How many of you have noticed the more you exert control, the more anger, rage, or rebellion you get back from your son or daughter?"

Ignoring Amashia's question, Damaris exclaimed, "But I thought it our duty to keep them from wrong behavior. This is almost more than I can hear!"

Suddenly Melita protested, "We are responsible for our children's safety and protection from evil. We are responsible for their shelter, food, and clothing." With this loud proclamation, a smug expression crept across her face as she saw others agreeing with her.

Amashia turned to the group asking, "So you agree with Melita the welfare of your children is your responsibility?"

"Yes! You know she is right," declared Shisha with more enthusiasm than usual.

Turning to Shisha, Amashia looked directly into her eyes. "Shisha, you have spoken for the entire group when you avow mothers are responsible for their children's welfare. Of course, we are responsible for our children's welfare. That is not what we are talking about here." She looked about until the murmurs stopped and then she continued to explain God's message.

"We attempt to control our older children to the point of using force because of our deeply ingrained feelings of responsibility. Teaching, encouraging, and trusting them to make good choices comes from loving the child and then accepted by the child in the manner given. Control implies a power we do not have when the child is out of our sight. When we try to control all areas of their lives, it prevents them from developing the ability to think and make decisions for themselves."

The women started murmuring among themselves. Voices reached a high pitch as the women argued among themselves regarding the true meaning of Amashia's message. Several cried out, "We must protect our children!"

"Yes," I thought, *"I agree. We must protect them."*

Amashia responded, "Let's slow down and see if we can understand the true meaning here without feeling threatened by this message. As mothers, we must define acceptable behavior; we must set limits; we must establish a spiritual code to live by. We will tend to their physical and emotional needs after we have done all we know to do, we must let go and trust them to make responsible decisions. Since we are all followers of Jesus, we need to pray for understanding the difference between controlling and guiding."

Melita spoke saying, "We have done things the same way for so long perhaps we can only see one way of mothering. Yet, we all feel we fail and fall short? If God has a different plan, and we refuse to explore it, what does that say about us as mothers?"

I was surprised to hear Melita speak up in support of Amashia's message.

"Amashia, if we change as much as you are asking us to, what will our husbands say? What will our mothers say?" inquired Claudia. "How will such a dramatic change affect our children?"

"Thank you, Claudia, for raising a valid concern. They will probably react much as you have; first with resistance, then understanding. This will be a subtle change as you will slowly be changing an inner belief. It is time to put aside our fears and our individual needs. It is time we put our children's needs first. Our children will not be equipped to live life as adults and fulfill God's desire for them if we have not allowed them to develop their God given abilities. Can you not see, in our attempt to perform our duty, we cripple them? In doing so, we prevent them from being confident enough to be victorious without us. To be successful mothers, we must raise our children to be responsible, triumphant and God-fearing adults without our smothering protection. Such protection would suffocate them until they either rebel, resent, or retreat."

The tension mounted. The women began speaking in whispers among themselves.

Amashia looked compassionately at each woman, her eyes begging understanding of the message. She questioned, "Does God control his children's choices and actions? If we look back at our ancestors, we can see where some would have been better off if God had controlled them. While he has the power to control them, he does not exercise control over them because it would break his law of free will."

Claudia began to speak hesitantly, as if from a far off place in her mind, "Maybe that is why Leah has no will of her own. I have felt so responsible; I made sure she did not fail at anything. I have always imposed my will on her. It breaks my heart to think I have injured her because of my desire to protect her."

Lovingly, Amashia went to Claudia, enfolding her in a gentle hug. She said to all of us, "We may find we have made mistakes out of our good intentions; however, we must remember we did not fail. We did not know a better way. I am standing before you today because God wants to enlighten us about what is best for our children." Amashia's kind words stopped all conversation. Everyone sat in quiet reflection.

Melita broke the long silence: "We believe we should have the ability to control our children. When we cannot, we think something is deficient in us."

"Yes, Melita," Amashia said. "We think we should be able

to control their destiny. Now we are learning control is not the answer.

"Now, let us look at shared responsibility. There are times when we must share responsibility with others where our children are concerned. We share our children's lives with the rest of our family, our children's friends, and the teachings of the priests. We are not their only influence. We all have to remember children have minds of their own. We can influence their thinking, but certainly can't control it."

Amashia continued, "We need to identify what we cannot control. Even thinking we have the power to control means we think we have power we do not have. Can we control our children when they are not with us?

"Not really. I certainly have no control over Eli," Naomi said.

"I found out I had no control over my daughter's decision to join the Essene sect," said Shisha.

"Please notice where you have genuine control and what it is like when you try to force your way on your child," Amashia instructed. "Condemning yourself for not knowing the consequences of what you have done when at the time you did the only thing you knew to do only leads to guilt. Forgiving yourself and doing what you now know to be right are necessities. I trust you to think deeply and prayerfully about this." Amashia paused briefly, and gazed compassionately at the troubled young women.

Forgive myself! The thought raced through my mind. I shuddered with the very thought of it. *I cannot even comprehend forgiveness because of what I did. It cost my son his life.*

With a nod to her maidservants, Amashia signaled them to proceed to their appointed places to serve the food. Amashia opened her basket of cool fig leaves carefully filled with the sweet dates and honey-covered figs. Pitchers of cool water filled the shallow bowls to quench the thirst of the women after their discussions.

Amashia waved toward the waiting refreshments. The chattering women drowned her spoken invitation as they exchanged questions and comments about the day's lesson. Even so, they moved toward the waiting maidservants and exclaimed at the variety of delicacies laid before them.

My eyes surveyed the beauty and energy of youth. Although some of the women's faces reflected worry or agitation, most were engaged in pleasant conversation. *"How easily we push God's teachings away and take up the familiar trivia of our lives,"* I thought.

With a start, I realized I harshly judged my valued friends for the very acts I had committed. Had I not lost myself in the menial tasks of gardening to escape facing God's will for me? My husband had become old without me noticing while I looked inwardly at my shame and guilt. The very real sorrow lodged in my heart at the death of my beloved son had escalated because of my guilt. At last, I acknowledged the selfishness of my actions over the past months. This searing self-condemnation allowed me to see how I had withdrawn from my responsibilities as a wife, a friend, and a member of Jesus' believers. Amashia's message had surely spoken to my heart, awakening me to how absorbed I had become in my own pain. I shuttered to think of my selfishness.

One of Amashia's youngest handmaidens quietly placed a delicacy-filled fig leaf and a cool bowl of water before me. She lightly touched my hand, and with a kind smile, she returned to her duties. As I reached for the cool drink, a wave of gratitude swept over me. How gentle and thoughtful this young follower

of Jesus treated me. Without urging, she saw my loneliness and
came to me with a generous act of kindness. Amashia's household demonstrated the qualities of followers of Jesus. The young
maid knew I was Judas's mother. Yet she gave me food and drink
for my body, sweet kindness for my soul, and accepted me without judgment. Marveling at her display of compassion, I sat in
solitary contemplation of

Amashia's message until roused by a touch upon my shoulder.

"It is time to return to our homes, Mary." Amashia nodded to
the waiting servants, holding the baskets containing the serving
pieces. To my surprise, all the women had left the court. Smiling
serenely, Amashia reached for my hand and led me away from
my hidden retreat.

Sleep would not come. I recalled Amashia saying control can
lead to rebellion. Suddenly, my heart became heavy when I realized how I had tried to control Judas. I felt certain the girl
he wanted to marry was not good for him. When I insisted he
marry the girl whom I thought right for him, he became rebel-
lious, and chose not to marry anyone. Weeping with regret, I
cried out, "Forgive me, Judas. My mistake in judgment robbed
you of a wife!"

Hearing myself say *"mistake in judgment"* caused me to sit upright on my mat. Could it be I was responsible for the act and yet
not be guilty? I had no idea my disapproval would cause Judas
so much pain. I had wanted to save him from making a mistake.
In trying to do so, I made a mistake myself. Yes, I was responsible.
The guilt came from condemning myself. All too often, I caught

myself doing that when I made mistakes. I thought, *"This teaching must be from the Holy Spirit. This revelation was a new thought to me.*

Zilpah studied me as we worked together in the kitchen. Sensing her eagerness to hear about our last lesson, I inquired, "Zilpah, would you like to hear about our lesson from Amashia?"

"Yes, very much," Zilpah replied. "I have been waiting patiently for you to divulge the understanding you gained today Mary, as I too am eager to learn."

"I admire you for your desire to keep learning. This lesson is a hard one to comprehend and embrace. We are to examine our need to control our children. God says this comes from a false sense of responsibility. We feel it is our duty to prevent our children from making mistakes."

"But we all want to prevent our children from making mistakes," Zilpah responded.

"Zilpah, remember when I prevented Judas from marrying the girl who had nothing to offer him; by insisting he marry the girl Simon and I had chosen for him? I am the one who made a mistake. As a result, he never married. I had no way of knowing my insistence would lead to a lonely life for him."

Trying to reaffirm my actions, Zilpah said, "Mary, we all felt the way you did about both women."

"Yes, we all forgot Judas had to live his own life. I think this idea is what God wants us to learn. In our culture, we have made those kinds of decisions for our children. It's time to change the way we see mothering and our children."

Sighing, Zilpah said, "Out of my sense of duty, I try to control my children's choices so they will not make mistakes. You offer me much to consider, Mary."

"For all of us, Zilpah. I hope to discuss this in detail with Amashia. Will you send Zeb to ask Amashia if she will come and visit with me about the lesson? I am still not ready to leave the house. She will understand."

The following day, I heard Amashia chatting away with her servants as she neared the kitchen path. Smiling, I thought about how she always came through the kitchen, usually leaving something delicious to eat. Zilpah welcomed her. As I entered the kitchen, Amashia raised her arms to receive a hug. "I am glad you wanted to talk with me," she said, "as I have wanted to talk with you, too."

"Let us go into the great room. It is too breezy in the garden today. Zilpah, will you bring us tea and some of the cakes you made yesterday?"

As soon as we rested on the couches, Amashia said, "I need to talk about the lesson too."

"What a relief, Amashia, knowing I am not alone."

"Well, I have been thinking about Shisha. She has always been an exemplary wife, yet her daughter seeks a far different way of life. I wonder how she can turn away from all her mother has planned for her, in order to live as an Essene in the wilderness. Do you think it's because of Shisha's controlling nature or because she feels it is God's plan for her?"

Milcah's thin, fair face and blazing zealous eyes floated before me. "Shisha does indeed have a controlling nature, but from what I learned yesterday, Milcah's reason for becoming an Essene does not matter as God gave her free will. Even if all of us think it is a mistake, it is her life to live as she wills it. We can pray Shisha comes to understand Milcah has free choice as an adult."

"Such wisdom, Mary. You comprehended the lesson in a deep way. I only hope the others gain this understanding as well."

Zilpah entered carrying a plate of cakes and tea for each of us. We both sat sipping our tea, not saying anything, lost in our thoughts.

Finally I said, "Melita loves her brood of children so much, and cares for them with enormous energy. All those young ones go around with sticky fingers as she shows her devotion to them by keeping their hands full of food. She does everything for them and participates in their every activity. Nevertheless, they are growing older now, and I wonder if she has begun to teach them to fend for themselves. Surely they will not feel capable of facing life outside her house until they learn to take care of themselves."

Staring off in the distance in deep contemplation, Amashia said, "What I saw as love before now looks like deprivation. Her insistence on doing everything for her children denies them the opportunity of developing a strong sense of capability and independence. Astonished, I realize in her loving desire to spoil them, she is keeping them helplessly dependent, a form of control."

"God is really opening our eyes," I responded. "These insights are foreign to our way of viewing motherhood."

"Oh Mary! How thrilled I am you are gaining a deeper understanding."

"And how thrilled I am you are providing these insights. I needed the understanding more than most."

Chapter 10

The Court of the Gentiles was a unique market serving all who came to the Temple. Pilgrims there could find food to tempt their whetted appetites, cloaks to replace their road-worn robes, sandals for weary feet, and all sorts of jewelry created to represent memorable images of the Temple. With great show, money changers haughtily picked their way through the rabble, carrying their precious bags of gold coins. Servants followed, tugging awkwardly on the heavy table and stool their master would set against the wall for his business. Voices cried out in protest as servants bumped unsuspecting shoppers in their haste to follow their snarling masters. The scene was loathsome to me. The false cheer and wheedling of the peddlers blended with the cries of jostled buyers. I found it sickening. I wanted to cover my ears, close my eyes, and flee from the court. It represented everything disrespectful and disgusting about the jealous priests and the empty rituals they performed.

My heart saddened when I considered the taint of worldly greed and jealously guarded power that invaded the original essence of the Temple. Had not these same priests, charged to preserve and protect the Holiest of Holies and led Judas to his dark deed? Surely, God's voice did not prevail in this sea of depravity. Amashia tugged vigorously on my hand to urge me past the discordant turmoil of the outer court.

As I looked upward, I saw the Roman guards on duty atop the high walls of the Fortress Antonia. They looked down upon the open outer court, noting every newcomer. The sun glinted on their polished armor, and I shuddered to think of the lives their sharp swords had taken. Simon's words of caution resounded in my memory and seemed prophetic. Were Amashia and I mad to think the priests would ignore defiance of the established ways? They were more likely to believe the words of a treacherous Roman official than those of God, spoken to a woman. A shudder passed through my body and I felt chilled, despite the warmth of my heavy cloak. I perceived Amashia's strength and commitment to God's work as more remarkable than ever.

Previously, I had thought Amashia's efforts were to lure me from my depression. Now I knew she had a far greater mission. God undoubtedly touched Amashia. With deep admiration for my lifelong friend, I quickened my steps, followed her into the quietest reaches of the Women's Court, and took my usual place.

When Amashia called to the group, she looked about acknowledging each woman with a welcoming smile. She asked, "What have you learned from our last meeting?"

"When last we met, you asked us to accept responsibility for our mistakes without self-judgment. I don't understand how this is possible," Alpheus said. "When we fail in our responsibility, guilt follows."

Amashia answered, "Not necessarily. The purpose of guilt is to get us to change our ways, not condemn ourselves. You surely remember when our Lord was on the cross he prayed, 'Father, forgive them for they know not what they do.' Those for whom he prayed were responsible for what they were doing. Yet they actually had no knowledge of their true actions. As mothers who feel so responsible, we have no actual knowledge of the damage we do. If Jesus forgave all those who were killing him, don't you think he will forgive us too, for not knowing what we were doing?"

"Of course he will," answered Sori. "The hardest part is forgiving ourselves."

Amashia picked back up saying, "We have to consider our tradition compelled us to tell our children what to think, what to do and how to do it. We did not fully realize how our over-mothering can create rebellion or squelch the divine nature of the child. Yes, we are responsible, just not guilty. Owning responsibility without blaming our self and changing the ways taught by tradition free us to be better mothers. Your burden will be lighter when your heart embraces this truth."

Esther spoke up. She said tearfully, "Because I controlled Salah when young, he is now acting out of control. He is not exercising control over his behavior." Sobbing, she continued, "I can see clearly how wrong I was. I never realized the damage I caused him by the shackles I placed on him through my excess control."

Amashia soothingly said, "I know the realization hurts. When you are responsible for unknowingly creating a weakness in your son, you did not have an inkling you were causing him harm. You desired to save him from mistakes. Perhaps you can consider discussing your actions and your intention with Salah. Ask for his forgiveness and tell Salah you want to help him learn to make responsible choices."

Claudia spoke up saying, "Esther, I feel as you do. I am heartbroken I made the same mistake with Leah. She has no will of her own."

My heart went out to both women as I felt what they both were feeling. Melita remarked, "This is a lifelong habit for most of us and will be hard to change."

"Letting go of control will be hard for all of us. Can you see the damage it does to our children?" Heads were nodding, including mine. Amashia continued, "For their well-being, we must make an effort to change our old ways."

All the conversations faded from my mind and switched back to, "Father, forgive them, for they know not what they do." I repeated this phrase. *Could it be true? Surely, Judas did not know when he identified Jesus the priests would conspire to yield him to the Romans. He would not have broken our Jewish law. He could not have known the gravity of giving Jesus up for public chastisement. Could he, too, be forgiven?*

When I saw Amashia rising to her feet, I forced my attention back to the message I knew forthcoming. Once again, she raised her arms high above her head and, gazing toward heaven, she paused as if in prayer. Lowering her arms, she carefully chose her words, beginning with, "My sisters, God has talked to us about false responsibility.

"Today, he wants us to understand our true responsibility. He wants to remind us he taught his children well, and always gave them free will. This is what he wishes for us to emulate. Hear his message.

"We mothers need to teach our babes God's ways from the time of swaddling. As understanding begins for the child, we must point out the natural consequences of departing from God's ways. Once a child understands what is expected of him, he is able to make a responsible choice. Once he chooses, we must allow him to experience the consequences of his choice. Consequences teach more than anything you can say. Some believe God punishes his children for their mistakes, while in reality, he allows the natural consequences of his children's decisions and actions to become their teachers. Experiencing the consequence teaches responsibility and accountability."

Shisha rose to her feet, crying out, "That seems cruel. After all, they are only children."

"I understand your reaction Shisha," Amashia continued, "Let's just think about this. If we protect our children from the natural consequences when they are young, how will they learn to take responsibility for their own actions? We need to let them experience the consequences when they are young, so they will become responsible when they become adults and the world holds them accountable. This is the best protection we can give them."

"Let's look even deeper. In seeking to protect our children from the ramifications of their choices, we have placed all the blame elsewhere. If we blame others and deny the child's responsibility, he cannot learn to develop responsible behavior." Amashia's voice rang out clearly and echoed off the marble walls of the Temple.

"My friends, our first responsibility is to raise our children to be responsible adults. We must see their behavior clearly and hold them answerable, as hard as that is to do." She studied the assembled women until she saw the round, serious face of Sori. "Sori, what is in your heart? Does God speak to you through these words?"

Glancing around the circle seeking disapproving faces, Sori found none and responded to Amashia with forceful confidence. "God is telling us our first responsibility is to teach our children his ways. Our children are to be able to serve him and care for themselves and others. They must learn the ways of the Lord to build their character and virtues. I can easily accept that. What I cannot grasp is allowing our children to experience the consequences of their actions. Our natural instinct is to protect them from painful consequences. With my husband gone all the time, I feel a greater sense of responsibility for meeting all their needs, including protection."

For Sori, this seemed a long speech and she almost collapsed back into her robe spread out on the sun-heated marble bench. She looked down at her clasped hands as though she should not have spoken up. Always industrious, Sori had little time for the squabbling and gossip of the young wives and rarely spoke in their presence.

The women echoed her sentiments. Alpheus could hardly speak as she stood saying, "Amashia, when you say we are to allow our children to experience the natural consequences of their choices, I am hearing you saying we are to allow our children to fail. I am afraid. My heart almost stops beating. I don't think I can do this."

With compassion, Amashia responded, "I know this will be hard as we have done our best to protect our children from the pain of their actions. Here are situations to help you determine if you are trying to protect your child or allowing them to experience the consequences of their behavior. Experiencing the consequences is the teacher of the lesson.

"What happens when your child steals something from another child? Do you try to excuse him? Or do you let him experience the natural consequences of stealing? If your child is caught doing something she should not do, do you blame someone else for her actions or do you let her experience the ramifications accompanying the action? Should your child become drunk, do you give him a strong lecture and then sooth him until he gets over it, or do you allow him to experience the discomfort of what drinking causes him? Can you not see when we protect them from natural consequences; they don't learn to take responsibility for their actions? Can you not see they will not be equipped to live in the adult world?"

"I can see that even though I don't want to accept it. This is the hardest lesson we have received," Sori moaned. "My desire to protect is so strong I don't know if I can carry this one out. With my husband gone all the time, I feel I must protect them."

Amashia sat staring down as if thinking. She raised her head and said, "Let us look again to God as our example. How has he dealt with his children?"

Naomi began to speak. "I have continued to think much about how God taught Adam and Eve. He instructed them not to eat of the tree of knowledge or they would die. He gave them choice, and then he allowed them to live with the consequences of that choice. They lost the ideal life with God as a companion and a lush garden in which to live. They had to leave the

Garden of Eden and work the hard ground among the thorns and thistles by the sweat of their brow. They also lost access to the tree of life to give them immortality."

Shisha said very thoughtfully, "We have heard stories from our ancestors proclaiming how much God loves his people, yet he has allowed them to experience the results of their actions. Remember how God warned the children of Israel not to worship false gods. Isaiah and Jeremiah cried out God's message for over 100 years! Yet when the people would not repent, God allowed them to be carried off into bondage.

"I see how we fail our children if we don't teach them the repercussions of their decisions. They must learn each choice they make will affect their lives and their future. At times their choices will cause them pain, embarrassment, or loss. These hard times will be their greatest teachers. Our children must understand every choice they make will work either for their good or for their detriment. Our task as mothers is to make sure they fully understand each choice has consequences for them. This truth will serve them to the end of their lives."

"We have heard the new lesson from God." Amashia said, "Naomi, Sori, and Shisha have given us thoughtful insights and appreciation for the earlier messages. Think on this when you go home and pray before the Lord. Let us refresh ourselves with food for our trip back to our homes."

I yearned to tell my household all I had learned. I wondered what Simon would think of all that had transpired in light of what I realized today. I longed to know his thoughts. At that moment, the huge gulf between Simon and me loomed in front of me once more. How could I possibly close the vast expanse between us? He had cruelly admonished me, and I had completely withdrawn from him. We had been absent from each other for well over a year now. Yet somehow, after all that happened making me apprehensive of approaching him, a warm feeling emerged in me at the thought of hearing his voice again. I grew sad thinking our pride might keep us apart forever. If only Simon could hear Amashia's message; nevertheless, how could he know of Amashia's lesson if I did not tell him?

The aroma of bread drifting from the house smelled so good to me it distracted my thoughts. Then the solution to my problem of approaching Simon became apparent. I had resumed my place within my household; now I wanted to regain my duties. I would once again assume the responsibility of a wife by serving my husband's evening meal. Even if we did not speak that night, I would still be in his presence.

I made my way to the kitchen. When I told Zilpah to prepare the dishes that I would serve Simon, she gently touched my cheek and looked at me as though she was pleased. Her warmth encouraged me as I quickly washed up and prepared to serve my husband after months of neglecting this duty.

Hovering about the kitchen, I made sure everything was just right. Feeling nervous, the thought of any of the food preparations going awry made my head spin. I wrung my hands and inspected every item the servants placed on the tray. I arranged and then rearranged the items, hoping to make the best presentation possible. I fussed over the smallest details. Yet I felt strangely comfortable — as if I had awakened from a bad dream and found myself again safe and secure. I knew tonight's dinner would not be the warmest nor the most comfortable, but I had to make this first step.

When I had assured myself everything in the kitchen was going as smoothly as possible, I went into the dining hall to make sure all was perfect in there. I rearranged cushions as I waited for Simon's return and thought of ways to approach him.

All too soon, I heard a servant opening the gate and welcoming my husband home. Hastening to the kitchen I made sure everything was in order for Simon's meal. With one last tug to straighten my tunic and adjust my girdle, I made ready to face my husband. With hesitant step, I entered the large hall.

Simon stood looking out the door toward the garden. His rigid stance indicated his eyes were not seeing the peaceful beauty of the scene before him. For the first time in months, I truly saw Simon. Shocked by the sight, highlighted by the last bit of sunlight, I stood still and stared. Belatedly, I realized how much sorrow he still carried. I hid so deeply within my own pain Simon had ceased to exist for me. This lonely man of thin frame and graying hair had replaced my vigorous husband, while I wandered lost in agony and remorse. How could we have drifted this far apart?

Without speaking to me or acknowledging my presence, Simon went to a couch and tiredly sank into it. He glanced at me when I knelt beside him to place his food and pour his wine. I could not guess his thoughts and his face gave no hint. With a weary wave of his hand, he signaled me to wait by him. With little appetite, he nibbled at the food before him.

Mustering my courage I began, "Simon, Amashia has been bringing us revelations on motherhood."

He did not look at me but kept his eyes on the tray of food before him for the longest time before he spoke. Finally, in a voice barely audible, he mumbled, "What kind of revelations, wife?"

His tone sounded cynical. I had expected his distrust, so my mind raced ahead to the mission God had given Amashia. I took a deep breath and hesitated before I said, "God wants to free mothers from accepting false responsibility for the actions of their children once they reach the age of account-ability. He wants to lift the burden of guilt from mothers for their adult children's actions. She is on fire with her devotion to this work." At last I caught my breath long enough to seek Simon's reaction to this news.

Avoiding me, he turned his face away through the open window at his side. Stillness filled the hall. It seemed inter-minable as I waited for his response. My mind raced through this unending pause. *Would he further admonish me for speaking of a woman's mission? Would he tolerate my interest? Would he con-tinue to be silent?* My heart began to pound in my ears while the silence stretched out.

His voice faltered as he continued, "And what does Amashia think the priests and scribes will make of all this?" Pausing and shuffling his feet back and forth, he said, "Has she considered husbands will not welcome changing the cus-toms of generations? A child's failure is evidence of our fail-ure." His words were again scornful. Yet another long pause felt suffocating to me.

Simon glanced at me briefly before looking away and say-ing, "What your dear Amashia suggests goes against all the ancient teachings and customs." After another deep silence, Simon turned a troubled face toward me. "Surely, she knows my name would no longer gain her honor and protection among the priests."

The realization of the disgrace Simon had endured emerged to the forefront of my mind. Filled with compas-sion, I realized I was not alone in my grief and shame. He endured it too, yet he could not hide from it. I could retreat within my home and hide in my chamber all day, but he must go into the marketplace and conduct his business. He had to hear the ridicule of the passers by and bear the silent disdain of the Temple elders. What I had only imagined I would suffer, he had experienced.

"I question this work." Simon furrowed his brow as he continued, "I don't doubt her sincerity."

I had wanted to tell Simon of today's lesson, but I could not bring myself to say more. His pain seemed too great. After gathering up the uneaten food, I took it to the kitchen. When I returned, Simon was sitting with his face resting in his hands. Since no one was present, he seemed to be talking to himself, saying, "I cannot ignore the ugly rumors spewing daily from the Temple. Even the Romans are in disagreement about Jesus' true identity. The smallest question of the high priests causes endless bickering and they become more vicious in their judgments with each passing day. They will not react kindly to Amashia's teachings. I am afraid they will claim it is blasphemy and have her stoned."

I was relieved to hear Simon express concern for Amashia. His caring self that I loved so much was back. Although he had expressed concern for Amashia's safety, strangely, I found myself feeling certain there was nothing to worry about.

♛

Chapter 11

The women arrived in the Women's Court of the Temple soon after Amashia had finished her meditations. Their eyes shone with a new eagerness to hear Amashia's profound teachings. The Court buzzed with their excited voices. After Amashia had brought order to the assembly, Lydia spoke first.

"I made the mistake of protecting my daughter Miriam and as you know, I am raising her children. I want her children to fully understand responsibility for themselves. I can see the wisdom of allowing our children to accept the natural consequences of their actions. They will be wiser if they know we will not protect them from the outcomes of their behavior. However, this is a very difficult thing to do. We cannot change all at once. To be fair to our children, we must prepare them for the change. First, we must teach our children every choice has a result. We have to let them experience even the small consequences of their choices. Sometimes they will be happy with the outcome, and sometimes they will be disturbed."

Shisha rose and addressed Lydia. "Thank you for answering my concern about how to start. I see we must be more concerned for our children's future than how we feel. They will be more responsible in making their choices when we let them know they will have to live with the fallout of their own choosing."

My heart raced as I realized Judas had made a choice he could not live with, so he took his own life. Tears streamed down my face as I wondered if I had overprotected him so he could not accept something going wrong. I wanted to scream and run from this place, but I knew I could not do that. The truth of this message had penetrated my whole being. Judas did not have the strength to face the consequences of his decision to turn Jesus over to the priests. My saving him from past mistakes must have contributed to his weakness. "Oh, forgive me Judas," I whispered.

My reverie was broken when Claudia, with her hand over her mouth, whispered, "Does this mean we are to allow our sons and daughters to experience the hurt of a bad decision?"

Placing her hand on Claudia's shoulder, Amashia said, "Yes, if we want to teach our children upright and Godly behavior, we must help them see the possible repercussions before they make decisions. If they decide to go ahead with their choice,

they will know they have to live with the aftermath. We must hold them accountable if they are to learn their lessons. We must think about the long-term effects on our sons and daughters rather than the current situation. If we start teaching them at an early age, then the consequences of their choices won't be severe or life threatening."

"So simple and yet so difficult," I thought. *"Stepping aside is not easy."*

Naomi ventured, "If I understand correctly, you are saying the most we can do is to teach our children how to make wise choices, and to teach them that every choice has a consequence they will have to live with."

Smiling broadly, Amashia said, "That's right, Naomi. You understand perfectly."

Alpheus spoke up: "When Naomi lamented her son's fascination with the harlots, I blamed his behavior on our city, full of temptations and wantonness. The examples our children get from some of the older men have not been good. I blame those men for influencing the younger boys."

Amashia responded, "The men will share responsibility and be held accountable for influencing the younger men. However, ultimately, Naomi's son still had a choice about whether or not he would partake in such behavior. Since he had a choice, he is accountable for his actions. Can we really blame others for our behavior when we all have freedom of choosing?"

Alpheus sprang to her feet, angrily shaking her finger in the air. "He would not have gotten involved if the older men had not shown him sordid and easy pleasure!"

Amashia calmly said, "You are right. However, all will be tempted. Even Jesus was tempted. Loving our children does not mean we must defend them or be blind to their flaws.

We must be willing to see them clearly if we hope to guide them.

"We know our city is full of people who provide bad examples. We must practice God's teachings and be the example Jesus taught us. In following the Master's example, our children will grow to be close to God and close to his teachings." Amashia's calm voice soothed the agitated women like a balm. They quickly diverted their gazes from Alpheus's flushed face.

"My friends," Amashia said, "God will help us become free and teach us our true responsibility. God has said we mothers have forgotten that our children are his children too. He wants us to look to him for guidance in raising our children. He dwells in each of our children and in us as well. His deepest desire is to guide us in the care of his precious ones. We need to surrender to his guidance."

"I am hesitant to ask," Damaris said, "if God dwells in my son, why is he drinking so much and fooling around with whores?"

"That is a legitimate question." Amashia said tenderly. "Now, I have a question for you. Does God intrude in any of our lives without an invitation?"

"Not really," mumbled the women.

Amashia continued, "Remember the many times Jesus said, 'By myself I do nothing. It is the Father in me who does the work.' He knew he needed to stay connected to God in order to fulfill his mission. We must all learn from him. We can be assured we need to depend on God to Guide us in raising our children. Since Jesus depended upon God for the ability to do his work. Trust God to help you and your children. We have only to ask for his guidance."

Finally, Melita drew my attention. Never known for her

shyness, she spoke with a tinge of defensive anger in her voice. "None of us has forgotten our children are God's children. God is supreme in our households." She looked about at the other women, who nodded rapidly. Melita continued, "We invited his son into our lives and into our homes. We believed in the Messiah before many in our city. We have not forgotten God's teaching or Jesus' example."

"That is very true, Melita. God is supreme in our households and we teach our children the way of the Lord. Here is a question we must ask ourselves, "Do I trust God to guide me and my child?" Silence fell among the group of women.

Lydia broke the silence. "I have pondered what has been said. I would say 'yes,' but as I think on it, I now am shocked to have felt all the responsibility. I am stunned to realize I had not trusted God to guide me. I never realized he would want to help me with my children."

Again, all the heads nodded in agreement that they felt the responsibility fell on them.

With compassion and understanding, Amashia said, "Let us remember if Jesus had to depend on God, then we too must rely on God for all we do, especially with our children."

Sori, who now sensed it safe to speak, said, "I would like to hear more about Jesus' statement, 'It is God in me.' I have never thought about God being in him or me. I thought I must always go to him as a supplicant." Her eyes sought Amashia's eyes.

"This is a new thought for most of us. We have prayed to a God far off. Remember when Jesus was among us, he went away to spend time alone with the Father. He sought God's counsel in all things. A short time before his death, he said he and the Father would make their home within us," Amashia replied, a different warmth glowing in her eyes.

"It will be hard to change the way we have always thought," Sori said emphatically.

"Once we accept that God resides with us, and we chose to ask him for guidance in nurturing our children, we will be surprised how fast change takes place," predicted Amashia.

After much discussion among themselves, Naomi's voice rose above the others. "This means if God's spirit is within us, he is within our children too. Our responsibility is to teach our children that God is with them. We must teach them to turn to him as they would to a trusted advisor. Like a close friend, they can tell him anything and he will help them. Every child needs to know that God loves her no matter what she has done or even thought of doing. Is this God's message, Amashia?"

"Yes! Oh Shisha, my heart swells with your understanding of this message," Amashia responded, touching her hand to her breast.

"In addition to turning to us, we are to teach our children to turn to God with their problems and concerns. God will help them see the right solutions and guide them through their troubles." Sori simplified Amashia's powerful message for all of us.

Amashia encouraged Sori, "We can depend upon God's guidance and so can our children."

My mind raced with the thought we could have God's spirit dwelling within us. Repeatedly, Jesus' words, "The Father and I will dwell in you," echoed in my memory. Only then did I begin to explore the true meaning of Jesus' words for his believers.

Questions swirled about in my thoughts. *Can God commune with us?* "Yes!" I answered my own question aloud. Stories passed from generation to generation of God's messages to our ancestors, flowed through the river of my memory. I remembered stories of God speaking to Abraham, Isaac, Jacob and Noah. Pensively, I searched for the accounts I had heard repeated since childhood. He spoke to Moses and led him to free our people from bondage to the Pharaoh. Later, he brought Moses to him on the mountain and gave him the Ten Commandments for his children to live by. Surely, the sages of old gained their wisdom directly from God. His son taught us to pray for wisdom as he walked among us.

I trembled at the thought. *Does this mean I, a flawed woman, can hear from God?* Even as the question formed on my lips, I knew his response. His assurance lay before me. I knew without doubt that he had spoken to Amashia. I heard many believers say Jesus first appeared to Mary Magdalene after his death. He spoke to her and called her by name for he knew Mary Magdalene.

My heart filled to overflowing as I considered the endless wonders revealed by Jesus. Hope flooded my soul as I thought his spirit dwells within me! I kept repeating his words, for they brought my Lord close to me again for the first time since his death.

My mind reeled in all directions while I tried to understand what this must mean for me. I got lost in my thoughts that day; I do not remember Amashia concluding the message. I do not remember leaving the Temple. I only remember suddenly being in front of the gate to my home. The refuge of the house of Simon seemed especially precious to me. My footsteps hastened as I saw the crisp cedars waving in a slight breeze, but I did not escape Amashia's scrutiny so easily.

She turned to me at the gate. "Mary, God has spoken to you today. I see in your eyes you are struggling with his message. Be as patient with yourself as he is with his children. Pray in solitude and await God's answers. God has a plan for you. Wait prayerfully for his words. I am only the messenger." With this mysterious statement, she hugged me closely and kissed both my cheeks. After one long look of questioning concern, she bade me farewell and hurried on her way. Her words echoed inside my head as I slowly walked through the shady cedar grove and onto the pathway to my door.

I went straight to my room to ponder all I had learned with the women. Overcome with hunger, I made my way to the kitchen passing through the great room where Simon sat looking out the window. Without changing his gaze, he asked, "Woman, did you join the women at the Temple today?"

Startled he had addressed me, I could hardly speak. "Yes," I murmured.

"What did dear Amashia have to say today?"

After a moment, I hesitantly said, "Simon you need not worry. We are not going to abandon our duties as mothers and wives; instead, we will be taking on new duties. God is teaching mothers how to raise Godly and responsible children. The priests have nothing to worry about, nor do husbands. Through God's teachings, women will become better mothers than ever before. God told us today we needed to seek his guidance as Jesus did when he taught and ministered. He also reminded us Jesus and he would make their home within us and within our children. We don't have to raise children alone; God's spirit within us will help us if we take time to become still and seek his guidance."

Simon continued to gaze out the window. After a while, he let out a long sigh and covered his face with his hands. "I have prayed and sacrificed many times seeking some solace from the burden of guilt I feel for Judas's betrayal of Jesus. Even so, I cannot rid myself of the plaguing questions haunting my nights."

The raw pain I heard in Simon's voice touched my heart. I knew that he spoke the truth. I reached for Simon's hand and held it in silence. Yet, I had no response for him. Our lives had been shattered. Perhaps we would have changed this had we been able to go through our pain together.

Nights were hard. I could not rid myself of Simon's tortured face as I tossed and turned on my mat. My guilt returned to rob my sleep. When I rose with the dawn, unrested and unsettled, I sought out Zilpah. I instructed her to resume the duty of serving Simon's dinner. I could not face his pain again.

Chapter 12

I had been working in my garden since early morning. All the flowers were brilliant from the early morning dew. Working in my flower and kitchen gardens provided the only comfort and peace I had found since Judas's death. I spent hours digging in the fertile soil. There I could unearth answers in my sorrowful search for peace. I thought of God's message brought to me through Amashia's lessons. My mind searched each word, attempting to understand God's true meaning and seeking the meaning it held for my troubled life.

As I tilled the soil and prepared it for new plants, I stayed focused on the messages we had been taught—we are to look to God as our model and teach our children his ways. I contemplated the fact that God had met with Adam and Eve and had walked and talked with them; yet they were disobedient. I dwelt on this scene until I could faintly grasp the message about false responsibility. They chose their will rather than the will of the Lord. Amashia's words echoed in my thoughts: *"We were no more responsible for the choices of our children than God is for the choices of his children."* I realized Judas had walked with Jesus. The Master himself taught Judas. Indeed, Jesus chose him, my Judas, as one of the chosen twelve! Even after being in close relationship with Jesus, he still chose his own way. If God's own son had been unable to influence Judas's decisions, then how could I have hoped to do so?

My mind continued to race with the lessons. There comes a time when every child has to accept responsibility for his own life; every one of us has the gift of free will. *Have we been trying to save our children from the natural consequences of free will?* When we depart from his teachings, we have the resulting consequence. The consequence then becomes the teacher of the needed lesson. *I always thought of negative outcomes as bad, not a lesson necessary to learn.* Jesus' teachings that God and he dwell in each of us was far more difficult to comprehend. I let that idea roll around and around in my mind hoping to grasp what this meant. *The message could only mean their spirit, their guidance, and their wisdom is available to us and to our children too.* I realized what I had done. I had blamed myself for Judas's death because I did not listen to him. I held myself responsible for Jesus' death because my son, Judas, betrayed him. For long over a year, I had convicted myself as the source of these unspeakable events. My heart began to race with the faint likelihood I might not be at fault.

I thought of all the women assuming guilt for the choices of their children, when in reality, I could see they were innocent victims of accepted tradition. I had been so numb with guilt and shame I couldn't reason for these many months. Encouraged, I discover once again that I could think with sound judgment.

Life began to return to me. Once more, my days were lived by decision and deliberate action. No longer did I wander aimlessly through my days with long absences from household activities. No longer was I a helpless victim of circumstance.

On the following morning, a grave sense of urgency awoke me. Filled with anticipation, I hurriedly readied myself for the day. Frantically, I searched my memory for some forgotten date or some omen to explain the solemn expectation permeating my being. Even after racking my memory for some clue, I could not shake the nagging feeling something important was about to happen. I met with Zilpah and planned the day's duties for the servants. Without returning to the kitchen, I hurriedly went into the garden hoping I could find relief from this pressing sense of urgency. I felt as if I were compelled to be in the garden, and no part of my home brought any sense of sanctuary from this forceful feeling.

Morning mist swirled around the trees, and dew trembled on the petals of the flowers. Sunlight had not penetrated the deep shade of my refuge. Furiously, I dug into the fertile soil preparing it for fragile new plants. I sought to lose myself in such menial labor. I wanted the smell of the earth to fill my nostrils. I wanted the warmth of the soil in my hands to stop the reeling of my mind. I felt frenzied and nervous, yet my mind could not find peace.

"Mary," a faint voice spoke. Surprised anyone would be about at this early hour, I rose and searched the garden. Seeing no one, I concluded my troubled mind played tricks on me.

With a twinge, I thought, *"Mary, you have lived within your cave of sorrow until you now imagine voices speaking to you from the trees!"* My hands shook as I resumed my determined digging in the soil.

Again, I heard a voice. "Mary, have you forgotten my love for you?" This voice became more persistent and I walked toward the door of the house expecting to see some long forgotten relative from my childhood or even, Simon. Once again, I could see no one in the garden. The doorway remained closed tightly against the early dampness. I remained completely alone.

"Mary?"

This time my heart leapt as I recognized the voice of the Master. Dirt clung to my trembling hands as I raised them in awe.

"Is it truly you, my Lord?" I whispered in amazement.

In the most tender voice, I heard, "Yes, my child." I felt the warmth of his presence as I had when he had walked among us. Gladness filled my heart. Then I remembered Judas's part in his crucifixion. I bowed my head and covered my face in shame and humiliation.

"How can you address me, Lord? I am so ashamed for my son's actions." I cried as the enormity of my failure swept over me. Tears wet the soil below my bowed head. I had caused my Master such agonizing pain.

"I know your heart, Mary. You have not failed me. Your shame and guilt have caused you to hide your face from me. I never left you. I have been waiting for your return to me."

His words filled my heart and made my load much lighter. "I have missed you so, my Lord," I wept brokenly.

"I have missed you too, Mary. You would not come to me. I was near you even when you felt most distant from me. Never am I far from you, my daughter."

I felt his sadness at my absence. "Ah, my Lord, I am so unworthy! I am so ashamed my son was the one who took your life!" I cried in sorrow.

"Mary, Mary, my life was not taken; I gave it. I gave it for you and all who need to be set free. My devoted child, you are free. I died on the cross so you could be free of all guilt and all shame. Do not let my sacrifice be in vain. I gave my life willingly and lovingly. And, as you can tell, I am still with you."

"Forgive me, Lord!" My body bent over in sorrow for my lack of understanding of his gift.

"Mary, I do not condemn you. It is you who judged yourself so harshly. My forgiveness has been here all along. You must receive it and in turn, refrain from condemning yourself. Only when you do this can you hear my message fully."

My bewildered mind swirled about me as I searched for meaning in his words. "Stop condemning myself?" I stammered.

"Yes, Mary, forgive yourself as I have forgiven you. You have judged yourself harshly for not listening to Judas on that fateful morning. Forgive yourself for not coming to me for comfort in your time of pain. Because you judged yourself so harshly, you closed your heart to my voice when I would have lifted you from your pit of shame and sorrow. You have sinned against yourself Mary, not me. There is no sin if you will accept my forgiveness," he patiently explained. I sensed his strength and reassurance just as I had when he stood among us.

Slowly, the acceptance and grace of God that Jesus described settled deeply into my heart. The love of God washed over me as waves upon the shore, leaving no trace of the refuse that littered my life these past months. Once again, I felt at one with my spirit and with my Lord. I remained kneeling in the garden enveloped in his love. In the stillness, my burden rolled away, just as the followers said the stone of his tomb had, and I rejoiced in the loving grace of my Savior. At last, I felt free from guilt, for he had reached me with his loving grace.

Springtime had come. As nature stirred from its dormant season and began growth anew, I found new life within myself. Finally, my life returned to some semblance of order. I was now ready to face my friends and make peace with Simon.

With my newfound peace came a resurgence of joy in the smallest tasks, the merest service to others. With a glad heart, I went about my daily tasks, reveling in my blessings and prayerfully asking guidance in all I did. As evening drew near, I asked God to give me the courage to share Jesus' words with Simon. Humbly, I asked for grace to be able to approach Simon in a way soothing to his troubled heart. I wanted to assure him this marvelous freedom could be his also.

As in that long-ago past, I chose to serve Simon's evening meal. Silently, I asked God to sustain me and to guide my words to Simon's heart. With a deep breath, I began. Although I had thought to approach my experience gently, my eagerness to share such amazing news caused the words to fly from my mouth like startled doves.

"While I worked in the garden this morning, I heard Jesus call my name!"

Simon tensed. When he neither looked at me nor spoke,

I continued. "Yes! He assured me he had never left me. He also told me our son, Judas, had not taken life from God's son. Rather, Jesus gave his life in order to fulfill God's plan for our redemption." With another deep breath, I stopped speaking. A frightening silence filled the hall.

Again, I prayed for courage and slowly told Simon of Jesus' words to me.

"Simon, we must remember Jesus taught Judas daily for three years. In our teaching of Judas, we did not fail any more than Jesus failed in his of Judas. Judas made his decision alone. We may never understand why it had to be he who did the deed that had to be done. I know all this is hard to accept Simon, but we must."

Simon nodded as if in agreement. I continued, "When Jesus was with us, he spoke of God's grace and forgiveness. I experienced his grace today. I had to forgive myself for not listening to Judas and for withdrawing from all of you. Never have I felt such love as I did upon hearing Jesus' tender voice of acceptance of me!" I bowed my head and waited for several long moments for Simon's response. When I could wait no longer, I said, "I must share this message with others."

Finally, Simon murmured something I could not understand. My strength failed me, afraid to ask him to repeat his response. After an uncomfortable silence, he said, "Mary, they may think you are just another grief-stricken mother and not a messenger of Jesus."

Unable to respond, I quickly left the hall, carrying serving trays as I went to the kitchen. I, along with Zilpah hastily prepared the remains of the meal for the beggars at the gate.

As night approached, I considered going to Simon's quarters. Afraid he would deny me entrance, I went instead to my sleeping mat. Even though Simon's reaction had not been the joyful recognition of Jesus' message for which I had hoped, I still felt a determination to share the abiding peace Jesus gave. My prayers were for Simon's doubts to dispel, and then prayers of thankfulness poured forth in profusion. My faith became stronger as I planned my next effort to share Jesus' words.

I lay upon my mat considering different ways to approach Simon as I anticipated the next day. Suddenly, I became aware of a light, filling even the darkest corner of my room.

Again, the voice of my Lord spoke. "Mary, you must talk about what you learned when you were holding yourself responsible for Judas's death and about what you have learned from me. You will deliver the next lesson to the women at the Court. Do not be afraid. I will give you words for your mouth and courage for your heart. You will not fear the rebuke of anyone, for I have touched you."

Could I really have heard the voice of the Lord? We had just learned God dwells within us and now I am listening and being directed by him! My heart thumped in my chest at the mere thought of standing before the women to tell my story. Bestowed with a great responsibility, there could be no turning back. The Lord had spoken.

Sleep came slowly. Upon awakening, I sent word to Amashia that Zilpah would accompany me to the Temple. I was ready to face all the women I had formerly taught. How could I fear earthly condemnation when Jesus had given me heavenly absolution? Even so, Simon's doubtful response forewarned me my testimony could be viewed as the rambling of a sorrow-crazed mother. Trembling, I knew I had to tell my story. In an effort to rebuild my confidence, I told Zilpah all that had transpired. She believed me with all her heart because she had seen the miraculous change Jesus' words had wrought in me. We arranged to meet Amashia at the gate of the Women's Court.

In my mind, I retraced the days since Passover, the fateful day of Judas's betrayal. Passover would soon be here again. How many times in the many months gone by had I been too numb to comprehend all that was happening, even when I could overhear people talking? How much of life had I missed before Amashia's visit to enlighten me about God's message to her? I had been eager to hear about the life I had missed during my withdrawal. Somehow, what she said gave me hope, even though at first it had been only a faint glimmer. I could understand how Simon had trouble accepting what I told him last evening. He had not heard the voice of Jesus as I had. How could he accept as readily as I could?

With careful attention to every detail, Zilpah prepared me for the trip to the Temple. She laid out my finest tunic and robe. She fussed with my hair until pleased with its shine and appearance. Eagerly, she awaited our departure to the Woman's Court.

My mind was preoccupied imagining the reaction I would face. I did not see my surroundings along our pathway. When we arrived at the gate, Amashia rushed to me saying, "Mary, God did not give me a lesson this week. As he professed in his first message to me, you are the chosen one among us."

"Amashia, the Lord spoke to me. He told me to deliver the message today. So much has happened. God's spirit is truly at work. Now I know how you must have felt the first time God spoke to you. You know my fears and doubts. Nonetheless, I am prepared. Jesus has given me direction." Humbly, I bowed my head.

"God is with you, Mary. Come with me. I will call the women to hear you speak God's desire for us."

Amashia took her position and raised her arms to bring a hush over the women saying, "My heart overflows with gratitude to God for answering my prayers. And, my dear friends, my heart overflows with love for each of you and for the honor you have shown me. My sisters, my delight in you grows as you are taking God's instructions into your everyday life and experience the truth in practice. We have been learning much from God and from his message to us. Let us again share our struggles and the insights of our hearts."

Naomi started to speak, but then choked with weeping. Everyone quietly looked away as she regained her composure. With quivering voice she began, "I am so ashamed. I find this hard to admit. I had quit trusting Eli and God. I lost faith in prayer when Eli continued to see the harlots in the center of the city. I trusted what I saw more than I trusted God. I acknowledge Eli is God's child. God has so much more power than I. God, forgive me for assuming false responsibility and for my superior attitude. I have made an oath to pray daily for God to bring Eli into his will. I also pray the Holy Spirit will intercede in Eli's behalf since I am not certain how to pray. I vowed to God to never give up on Eli." Tears flowed freely from her sorrowful eyes.

"I never thought Naomi would relinquish her control. God must surely be present," I concluded.

"Naomi," Amashia said softly, "God has reached you deeply. What a witness you are to the presence of God to have gained this knowledge. Your persistence in prayer is like Hannah's, the revered mother of the prophet Samuel. Hannah, without child for many years, finally cried out in desperation for God to give her a child. She too, made a vow. She dedicated his life to the Lord. Think of the blessing Samuel brought to our people. Let Hannah be your guide in prayerful perseverance. So you see, Naomi, God does answer a mother's heartfelt prayer. God will hear your prayers for Eli. We must trust God to do the work in him."

The women's voices rose with assertions they would support her vow.

"I have realized I am not doing my children a favor by anticipating their every need and doing everything for them," Melita broke into the babble. "I know now they will not be able to make good choices as adults if I continue to protect them from life. I only hope it is not too late."

"Melita, it is never too late." Amashia gently embraced her.

Alpheus had avoided discussing her problem with her son, Nahor. She surprised me when she spoke up.

"Nahor has had a nasty temper all his life. I have defended him by blaming others for his sour moods. I have failed my son by doing this. He even blames me for his inability to form friendships. By blaming others, I have taught him to use blame as an excuse for not assuming responsibility. I failed my son." She hid her face with trembling hands.

Amashia asked, "How many of you find it hard to tell your children when you have been wrong?"

The women were silent and intense.

Amashia continues, "Alpheus, while it hurts to realize you made a mistake, explain to Nahor that you were wrong to blame others for his behavior. Help him to understand he and he alone is responsible for every thing he does or does not do. Nahor is smart, and he will learn he can become a better person and a happier person when he accepts responsibility for his own choices and actions. Our responsibility is to make sure our children achieve responsibility for themselves. That may not seem like a gift to our children at this time; however, over time it will prove to be preparation for successful adult living."

"No, it certainly doesn't seem like a gift today," Melita quipped.

"God is not condemning us for our mistakes in judgment," Amashia continued, "we must forgive ourselves when we have been wrong. God is blessing us for our efforts made in misguided love. He will light our path to his will."

One by one, each mother poured out her heart. The changes in them became visible. God's Holy Spirit worked in each woman removing their misperceptions and replacing their erroneous thinking with God's desire for them. My heart overflowed with love and compassion as I listened. God's presence was evident in the sympathy and support the women gave one another. Each woman shared what she had learned about motherhood. My heart pounded because now I must tell my story.

Chapter 13

O nce again, Amashia stood saying, "Oh how I celebrate your awakening and your enlightenment. My heart is full of gratitude to God and to each of you. You are not alone in this awakening to a better understanding of your role of mothers. As you recall, I sought God's help for our friend, Mary. As we all know, Mary withdrew from us and from the world when Judas and Jesus died. While she has been with us at each meeting, she could not face you with her guilt and shame until today."

The women looked at each other quizzically wondering how

I could have been with them. Amashia answered their look by saying, "Mary will come out from behind the great column where she has been hidden. You have helped her understand herself through sharing your problems and concerns. God has spoken to me, and God has spoken to Mary. He wants her to tell you her story. She will bring the message God has for you." Amashia came to me, took my hand, and led me into the midst of the startled women.

I took my position and dropped my veil, no longer needing to hide. "My dear sisters, for many years I have been your teacher along with many women in our city. I stand here today, not as your teacher, but to share humbly what you have taught me. I thank each of you for your receptive spirits and humility before God. Your insights have done much to help me heal. I am grateful to each of you."

The women sat spellbound, not moving or saying a word.

"I have been an example not as a mother, but as a woman who would not hear God. I had taken full responsibility for the deeds of my son, Judas. You are looking at a mother, through the grace of God, is free from the burden of guilt and shame."

Sighs of relief could be heard from the small group.

"I have carried this burden of failing as a wife and mother for these many months. I also thought I had failed you as your teacher. Others, including my husband Simon, have believed the same. Believing I had failed our Lord, I withdrew from everyone." The women became very still, totally focused on what I had to say.

I continued, "Through God's miraculous words delivered by Amashia, I am reminded I was not Judas's only teacher. Our Master also taught and influenced Judas. Judas knew Jesus well.

He walked with him and saw him teach and heal many others. Judas made his own choice; those choices not only brought him excruciating pain, but also brought pain to those of us who loved him, and to fellow believers. His choices even affected the lives of many others outside our realm. I have learned from listening to each of you, whose love for your children is great, that children will make poor choices, even with the best of parents. As difficult as it is for me to accept, Jesus told me he gave his life to fulfill God's purpose."

With a deep breath, I began to tell about my experience of Jesus' visit to me. His grace transported me beyond self-consciousness and filled my voice with awe. "While I was working in my garden, Jesus spoke to me. What a wondrous experience of love and grace! Jesus asked me to share his message of freedom from guilt and shame we now enjoy by his act of sacrifice. He wants you to know the pain, loneliness, and isolation we bear when we carry unwarranted guilt or shame, separating us from the Lord when we most need him. Regardless of what you have done or failed to do, God never abandons us. He never left me; I left him causing our Lord pain. My mistake seemed greater than those others could ever make, but only because I told myself so. Because I thought I made a horrendous mistake with Judas, I would see none of you, which caused some of you pain. It felt like death to me, yet I still breathed.

"Because I had condemned myself so harshly, I learned from Jesus that I had to forgive myself as he forgives all who ask for forgiveness. Without forgiveness, we separate ourselves from him and from each other. Jesus told me how my being away so long saddened him. Because of his love and grace, I am free today, and so are you. I ask you now to forgive me for withdrawing from you and for refusing to hear your sweet pleas for my return."

Almost in unison, voices cried out, "Of course we forgive you! Forgive us too, for giving you up as lost!"

"Thank you, my sisters. We are all in the one family of God. Your demonstration of love and forgiveness has touched me deeply. I will make every effort to reconcile with Simon too."

"There is yet one thing the Lord wants me to tell you. He wants us to continue to meet in order to give each other encouragement as we continue to understand our roles as mothers. I will be here, not as your teacher, but instead so I might learn along side of you." I concluded bowing and touching my head, mouth, and heart, as custom decrees to indicate, "My mind, my words, and my heart are here to serve you."

The women moved near me, and Naomi reached out and took my hand. With compassionate eyes, she pulled me close in an affectionate embrace. She embraced me as she would a long-absent sister, kissing both my cheeks. Others reached out to me, and soon warm hands clasped my trembling cold ones. Tears of thankfulness for their kindness filled my eyes. These dear women glowed with God's love and with love for one another. At last, I laid aside my guilt and shame. My strength and determination no longer turned inward with self-loathing. Jesus' voice had called to me in the darkness of self-pity and brought me to this place of loving light. His message led me to a fierce longing to serve these precious friends with the same fidelity with which I served him. For the first time, I glimpsed the merest understanding of Jesus' words, "Even as you do to the least of these, you do to me."

My first step along the path he had shown me was a new beginning. I felt as if Jesus spoke to me again. Without conscious deliberation, I knew I must reconcile my heart with Simon and with Judas's spirit. No room for doubt or recrimination existed. The time was long overdue for me to bridge the gap of estrangement and hostility separating me from Simon. Jesus had moved the women to forgive me of my past prideful boasting and present withdrawal. He would guide me to remove the barriers of blame and denial separating Simon from me. I felt an assurance of my Lord's presence as real as if he had touched me. He was near. Had he not reassured me in my garden he had never left me? His presence felt so real; I so fully expected to see him. I looked about for him.

Still bathed in the warmth of the women's loving friendship, Amashia and I made our way home. How joyous we were in the afterglow of seeing those mothers accept the essence of God at work in our lives! Our hearts were light and full of hope for the future. We contemplated about each mother's acceptance of her true responsibility and rejection of her false responsibility she had accepted in the past. Certainty of God's omnipotent presence in each child erased our last doubts.

Amashia's effervescent sense of humor brought laughter to our deep reflections. "Imagine Nahor with a smile as sweet as honey! He will be a handsome young man once he learns to spread his lips in the sweetness of a smile instead of puckering them in the sourness of a pout!" As she ended her musings, she comically puckered her full lips and then smiled broadly.

"Ah, I can hardly wait to see the young maids casting their eyes on him!" She clasped her hand to her heart in the manner of an infatuated young maiden. Thus, we made our way through the familiar streets. Ours was a happy group of true believers. The very essence of Jesus' love moved each of us to a new level of being. As when he had walked among us, his presence of spirit brought a lightness of heart and happy laughter to our lips.

As I lay on my mat cherishing the wonder of this day, I recalled the recent vivid dream, which had revealed the multitude of women to me. I was puzzled then, as now, to see such diverse women, many not of our land. Some seemed sad or in pain; each seemed to seek something from me.

"My Lord, reveal to me the meaning of this dream. I cannot interpret the vision you have sent me," I prayed.

In the quiet, I heard his gentle voice answer my plea: "Mary, in your dream, I was preparing you for the work I have for you to do. Many mothers need to hear what you have endured and what you learned from your experience. Your life will bless mothers for generations to come. Your story will give hope to those who suffer as you have suffered and prevent many others from making the mistakes you made. You are my messenger to those to whom I have entrusted my children. All mothers must know I will help them care for their children's earthly needs as well as for their soul's needs. They need only ask, and they shall receive my guidance."

"You have blessed me richly, my Lord. My heart is touched with your mercy and your love. I am humbled to be your servant." Tears of joy wet my face.

"Thank you, Master for hearing my prayers. You live within my heart." With this acknowledgment of God's blessing, gratitude and joy warmed me as I slipped into blissful sleep.

Chapter 14

My reconciliation with my Lord and my friends had brought me relief. Now I wanted to make peace with Judas. "Zilpah, it is time for me to go once more to my son's grave."

She placed her hand over her mouth and shook her head from side to side with fear in her eyes. "No, mistress, please don't go. You have only now turned away from the darkness of that awful place. Wait until Simon can take you there. I beg you, do not return there."

"My cherished friend, you need not fear for me. I must go

alone and make peace with Judas. Simon and I have spoken of that dreadful day and my refusal to hear Judas. My heart is still heavy because I did not listen to my son. He tried to tell me of his betrayal of Jesus, and I closed my ears to his plea. I must tell him how wrong I was dear Zilpah, and the depth with which I forgive him and ask his forgiveness." Her disapproval was plain; yet she busied herself with preparations for my visit to the field now known as the field of potters.

We walked through the crowded streets. The pungent smell of dung from camels, horses, and asses mixed with traces of aromatic spices and familiar vegetables heaped upon the beasts. Noise came from the animals and their handlers. Loud calls of traders hawking their goods to households behind high walls stabbed the dusty air. My young male servants walked before and behind Zilpah and me to protect us from the touch of the unclean, jammed by the stream of people rushing toward the markets in the center of Jerusalem. For once, I felt a twinge of envy for the comfort of the Roman women borne in litters upon the shoulders of slaves. Protected from the swirling dust behind curtains, they rode above the stifling stench-filled streets. Caught in this torrent of humanity, we were much like leaves carried in the rushing river waters. We could not have turned back even if we had wished to do so.

Soon we passed the pandemonium of the food market and went through the busy, but quieter, quarters of the artisans. Our steps quickened to the beat of the ironmongers' hammering. At last, the clanging blows were behind us and the lesser gate, allowing us to pass out of the city, stood before us. The high, solid, gray stone wall surrounded and protected all who passed within.

Scribes and elders sat in small groups offering guidance

and settling disputes. Sturdy Roman soldiers in full battle regalia challenged all who entered and left the city. Donkeys, horses, and camels pawed the stone pavement and protested their burdens. We rapidly left the press of the city behind us. Shortly, the field of the potters came into view.

I gazed at the straggling trees on the edge of the ravine remembering Judas's distorted body in the terrain below. My heavy heart flooded my eyes with tears. Silently we continued to a lone fig tree overlooking the desolate field where Judas lay.

"Please wait here. Refresh yourselves beneath the shelter of the fig tree. I must go on alone," I bade my small band of servants. Zilpah's hands touched my shoulders. She gazed deeply into my eyes. As if she discerned the purpose in my soul, she kissed both my cheeks and gently turned me toward the rough path. Slowly, I made my way between the brambles and over the rough ground.

All too soon, I stood in the field where Judas's shallow grave lay. How my soul grieved my son buried in this desolate place, filled with the sorrows of the lonely and forgotten. I fell to my knees and placed my hands over the barren soil where my son lay cast aside. Although thorny weeds grew in abundance in the sun-baked field, no seed had sprouted over Judas's body. The cruel sun had baked the red clay to a hard crust. The sun and rain had combined to entomb Judas as securely as stones. After a time of recalling Judas's face as a child, I forced my memory to our last meeting. My words came haltingly to my lips.

"For these many months, I could not come to you, my son, for the chains of shame and despair held me in bondage. Judas, the Master came to me and told me you did not take his life. He willingly gave his life to fulfill the Father's plan for our salvation. His words of assurance have freed my soul from guilt.

149

Only now can I see the trust and honor you paid me that fateful morning when you turned to me in your anguish. I ask you to forgive me, my beloved son, for failing you in your hour of need. Your burial in this lonely place grieves me. Your father's pain moved him to deny you burial in his family tomb. Yet, he too has suffered greatly from your loss, our only son. We now know we cannot erase that bitter night for any of us. We grieve for you, my son."

Warmth from the earth spread into my trembling hands. Tears of release fell upon Judas's grave. My throat seemed choked with sorrow for the lost promise of Judas's young life. Brokenly, I continued, "Oh, Judas, my precious son, I am still troubled as I remember gazing upon your face after your soul had departed." My body wrenched in pain as I allowed the sorrow and grief to pour forth in cleansing tears. "I do not know why you chose to be the betrayer. Nor do I know what you required of me that fateful morning." I waited as if I would get answers for my troubled heart. After what seemed like an endless time, my tears finally ceased. "Judas, Jesus reminded me he died so all could be freed from the guilt they carry. I pray your soul has found mercy. Forgive me Judas for not listening when you turned to me in your hour of need. I deeply regret my denial of your confession and my refusal to hear you. Another thing troubling me is trying to force you to marry the girl not of your liking. And please forgive me for that also."

I bade Judas farewell. Rising from the earth, I looked toward the distant fig tree. Quickly, I walked to my waiting servants. My mind turned to my husband, Simon. *Somehow I must reconcile with Simon.*

A sound above me drew my eyes to the clear sky. A lone white dove soared over the ragged ravine. In my turning to bid

Judas farewell, it seemed as if that dove carried my burdens away with her as she banked homeward in the cloudless sky.

The following morning, I rose with renewed energy and went about my duties of tending my husband's morning bath and dress. How good it felt resuming my former routine.

Simon's brisk pace and his step seemed lighter as he left our house that sunny morning. I smiled, realizing as I healed Simon also healed. Zilpah came to speak to me, and we moved about the house. Once again, I was the mistress of my home. Zilpah's obvious relief at my return to my responsibilities was evident in her many comments regarding the small daily tasks of caring for Simon's large house. I went about the house as a stranger seeing it for the first time. Its beauty and serenity touched me deeply. I felt a surge of appreciation for Simon's position reflected in this comfortable house.

I regretted the many months of silence invading our home, which once welcomed and entertained our friends and strangers from afar. No more was his door open to visitors from all corners of the earth. No more did his laughter ring out at the amusing stories of fellow merchants. Gloom darkened a house once filled with light and laughter. In the quite solitude no more did he tell of his son Judas and his devoted service to Jesus. Sadness flowed through me as I gazed at the silent scene of past pride and pleasure. I knew then the time had come to move on with our lives.

The meal was so important to me; I carefully planned every morsel placed before Simon. After months of allowing Zilpah to manage the kitchen, I enjoyed my responsibilities as a wife. Although the servants said nothing about my unexpected presence among them, they exchanged many smiles and nods. Never had they been more willing to do my bidding as they recognized my happiness. An air of festivity soon entered the house.

Copper pots glimmered in the firelight. I carefully arranged figs, dates, and grapes on our cherished alabaster platter. Simon enjoyed fruits with his first bowl of wine and I wanted him to begin his meal with pleasure. The aroma of roasting fowl wafted from the spits in the outer yard.

Zilpah crushed garlic with her small stones and placed it in the earthen jar containing lentils. She turned her attention to a young girl who prepared Simon's favorite vegetables. The hearts of palm, cucumbers, and mushrooms were soaking in a large earthen bowl filled with vinegar and seasoned with salt. A large carved wooden platter of vegetables arranged in colorful rows displayed the beauty of nature. Our elderly manservant tended the glowing coals, slowly parching the grains of barley and lightly sprinkling olive oil over them. I secretly watched the girl's work because Simon did not like oil to drip from his fingers as he ate. Both Zilpah and I kept a close watch on the busy kitchen. After my absence, the homely tasks seemed exciting to me. Simon's pleasure and his comfort in his home were again my cherished pleasure.

"This is like a wedding feast!" cried out a young lad as he poured water from a large pitcher. Firelight danced on his innocent features. His words were truer than he could ever know. This night I vowed to approach Simon as a new wife for the second time.

"Mary, the evening meal is ready for your husband. Your flowers are in the hall. Do you wish anything more?" Zilpah asked.

"No. This evening I will wait upon my husband as he takes his meal. I want no one else in his sight. No ears but mine shall hear his voice."

Zilpah's glance mirrored the swirl of feelings in my breast. Her eyes bespoke joy that I again lived and yet apprehension Simon might not receive me. Our eyes met in silent understanding. With a quick adjustment of my robe, she nodded and returned to the kitchen.

Time seemed to stand still as I moved through the halls, awaiting my husband. I had been unaware of my surroundings. Now I could see our inviting home with gratitude for the first time since Judas's death. My mind turned to the first time I saw the house Simon had built for me—strong and beautiful, away from the hustle and bustle of the streets. What excitement I felt that day and how happy I was to be his wife. The smooth white walls gleamed in the last rays of the evening sun. Tiles laid in intricate patterns stretched before me in the halls. Beautiful, brightly colored mats lay ready for guests' comfort. The low tables used for serving bowls and pitchers were richly carved. Every doorway had artistic sills bearing blessings of the prophets. Rich red curtains hung on the walls. Cedar lattices covered the high windows. Sweet fragrance wafted into the rooms from the lush plantings in the courtyard. Every room serenely invited those who entered to find rest and repose. He built this house to receive me, his bride. My heart leapt to my throat as I at last grasped how much he had done to prepare for me. Tears tumbled on my lashes as I gazed about me. My heart ached to think of the loneliness and sorrow Simon had borne alone. Once again, my heart overflowed with love and compassion for him. He could have put me away from him at any time during these past months for my isolation. Hope welled within me. *Surely, I can win my husband's trust once more.*

Anxiously, I awaited my husband's step on the outer courtyard. My hands trembled and my brow became damp. At last, I heard his heavy tread. Having sent the porter to the outer gate, I pulled the heavy cedar door open before he reached the portal. His eyes showed surprise, but he uttered not a sound. Wearily, he shrugged out of his dusty mantle. As I knelt, removed his sandals, and bathed his feet, he gazed above my head. Even this lowly service to him brought no acknowledgment.

Despite Simon's coolness, I gently requested, "Please, my husband, come into the dining hall. Your evening meal is prepared and awaits you." I walked briskly to the room where I had laid out his wine bowl, fruit, and roasted barley a short time before. I did not realize I held my breath until Simon entered the room. With relief, I gave a great sigh.

Simon reclined and began to sip his wine. Modestly, I knelt beside him and lifted a fig to his lips. After a moment's hesitation, he allowed me to place the fruit in his mouth. Puzzlement showed in his frowning face. Looking at him closely, I gasped at the deep lines creased his brow and the white gleam of his hair. Tentatively, I touched the snowy curls of his beard. Tears rolled down my cheeks, for I knew I had been part of his burden, just as he had been a part of mine. Those tears seemed to wash away an invisible curtain between us.

Hope sprung forth that Simon and I would be husband

and wife again. "Wife, I hunger after a day's fast," Simon said, looking at me. My heart raced with happiness as I left to bring the special meal we had prepared for this evening.

The fate of our household seemed to rest upon this meal and all sensed it. There had been none of the usual chatter among the servants when I took the bowls from Zilpah.

His dark eyes did not look away as I entered, but watched silently as I walked to him and placed his food before him. He began to eat. With deliberate movements, he tasted the fowl, the vegetables, and the freshly baked bread. He cleared his throat and spoke in a soft voice, "Mary, will you take food with me?"

"Yes, my husband, I will take food with you," I said.

"Eat of the meat, for you have grown thin these long months gone." He broke the leg, my favorite piece, from the fowl and held it out to me. His hand trembled as I took the food from him. We ate the meal in a silence that no longer seemed fraught with fear.

When Simon had eaten, he stared quizzically for a moment, "Will you join me in the courtyard?"

"With pleasure, my husband," I quickly responded. We rose from our mats and I followed him into the cool dusk. My heart lifted as he slowed his step so I could walk beside him. We strolled in the garden I had so carefully nurtured, even during my darkest days.

I began to speak haltingly. My heart felt it would burst from my breast as I said softly, "Simon, I am so sorry we withdrew from each other these past months when we needed each other as never before. We each had enough to bear without adding to each other's pain. I hope you can find it in your heart to forgive me. You have suffered shame and humiliation too. I now under-stand much of what drove you to express the harsh judgment of me when you learned of Judas's betrayal. Out of my love for you, I forgive you, my husband."

I slowly raised my eyes to see tears sliding down Simon's cheeks. Very gently, I continued, "God does not hold me or you responsible for Judas's deed. Judas chose his own path. We may grieve for his choice and the pain it caused, but no longer can we blame ourselves." We stood near each other in a peaceful silence.

"Oh, Simon, I have so much to tell you about the last few days. Please come, sit with me on this stone bench as I recount all that has happened." Reaching out to take his hands in mine, I said, "My husband, I want to tell you of the wondrous teachings God has given us through Amashia." Simon gave me his full attention.

In my passion, I had grasped Simon's hand to my breast. Imploringly, I gazed into his face. Suddenly, his features clouded and he began to sob, "Mary, oh, Mary! You have come back from the darkness. God has sent us this message of forgiveness so we can go on living. Are you certain? Did you and Amashia truly hear the voice of God?"

"You speak the truth Simon; I am back from the darkness. Yes, we did hear from God. For such a long time, I had wandered away from you and away from God. I am here with you now."

"Mary, we have lost Judas, but let us not lose each other. We shall make our lives as a clean tablet and write an end to the pain we have brought each other."

Simon's words were few, but they swelled my heart to bursting. I took his hand, we rose, and strolled among the fragrant flowers, each of us lost in our own thoughts. Soon the evening cooled and Simon walked toward the entrance to the hall.

"Mary, will you attend me as I prepare for sleep?" His face softened when he saw my willing smile. We walked to his chamber without another word.

My hands were clumsy as I carefully placed Simon's sleeping mat. I felt as timid as a young bride would. It had been so long since Simon had received me here. The water for his evening bath seemed heavy in the jar. As I struggled, Simon took it from my trembling hands and bade me rest on his mat. I watched him complete his bath and walk toward the small lamp glowing beside the door. He bent and extinguished the flame. I sat very still, hoping he would not send me away. He stood before me while I gazed upward, daring not a word. Slowly, he knelt before me and took my face between his palms.

"My wife has come home from a long journey. I shall welcome her with gentle caresses and warm kisses."

With these few words, he ended our separation. Never had a bridegroom welcomed a bride with more passion. Never had a bride opened her arms more joyously.

When we had shared our bodies to exhaustion, I laid my head against Simon's strong chest, heard his steady heartbeat, and drifted into a dreamless sleep. For the first time in many months, I slept without tears and without waking.

Morning found me clasped tightly in my husband's arms. My heart sang with gladness as my body and soul began the journey toward renewed life.

Epilogue

There I sat in the doctor's office waiting my turn to see the doctor. It had been a little over a year since the accidental death of my older son, David. Neither grief therapy nor time helped me heal. In fact, I had become progressively worse. I realized the time had come to seek professional help. After the doctor took a history and did an exam, she stood before me, hands on her hips, and curtly inquired, "What are you feeling guilty about?"

A flood of tears followed. Guilt was buried so deeply in the caverns of my soul; I never recognized its existence. Even then,

I could not identify the source; however, the tears had revealed the definite presence of guilt.

That experience marked the beginning of a journey to heal my soul. My research on guilt revealed the subtleties, often buried so deeply within, we are not conscious of them. Through adoption, David fulfilled my dream of motherhood. Picked to be his mother from among the other couples who wanted him, I felt especially blessed. As a result, I developed an unhealthy sense of responsibility for the quality of his life.

Having served as a human growth educator and professional speaker for more than twenty-five years, I was keenly aware of the many women who shared their experience of motherhood and the guilt they carried over their children. These mothers could not recognize the difference between false responsibility and true responsibility; now, I discovered I was one of them.

The idea to write this book began over dinner with my good friends, Adele and Stephen Farrell. After mentioning I had been contemplating the ramifications of motherhood and what it would have been like to be the mother of Judas Iscariot, Adele suggested I write a book on "The Judas Mother Syndrome."

What a privilege it has been to share Mary's story with you! When I started the story, I was still in a state of woundedness. Out of the ten-year process of research and writing (and the many rewrites), a great healing and freedom has evolved for this author.

I have spoken to you from my heart. It is my prayer your heart will be open for whatever the story holds for you, especially freedom from maternal guilt and help for young mothers raising self-responsible children with deep spiritual roots.

~~※~~ *Bobbi Sims*

Acknowledgments

I gratefully acknowledge all the supportive professionals, loving friends and family who helped bring this book into being. It not only takes a community to raise a child, it also takes a community of people to birth a book.

I extend my heartfelt gratitude to Libby Vernon, Ph.D., for her research on the historical times, for her creative contributions, for her ability to jump start me early on, and for her enthusiasm for the need for the message.

My immeasurable gratitude to my process editor, Audrey

Ellzey, whose ingenious insights and brilliance guided me to clarify my message. Audrey challenged me to work with the book to attain its highest potential. She became a wonderful coach, teacher and friend.

I am deeply grateful to Debbie Sewell, for her gentle spirit, for her research on parenting, and for her splendid suggestion to write a companion workbook adding an important new dimension to the work.

In loving gratitude to Cherry Williams, with her banister-questioning mind, and whose exceptional discernment and sensitive comments were always on target. Her final insights added the crème de la crème.

My deep appreciation to Diane Bates, M.ed and Kenneth Smith, M.ed, grammarians par excellent, who made this book a much better read.

Thanks to Sheri Phillabaum, Ph.D. Her insight for taking the story and staging the performance won my respect and appreciation. Her enthusiasm and encouragement about the performance added a new dimension to the original work.

Thank you Joan Jensen, LPC, for your loving support and belief in this work. You were a great encouragement to me.

To my readers: Carol Casper, Jim Cottingham, M.D., Ruth Kane, Katherine Williams, Billye Williams, Janet and Buz Maxwell, Scott Smith, PhD., whose enthusiastic comments and loving contributions have touched my heart in a profound way, thank you so much.

For those souls who have supported me in the office during this project, I am most grateful.

I especially acknowledge those close to me who tolerated my dedication to the work, who believed in its message, and who gave me encouragement along the way. To my friend, Janice

McAfee, my very special gratitude. To my friends, Annette, Carol, Janet, Richard, Steve, and my encouraging clients, I love you all for cheering me on.

Coming Soon

Overcoming the Judas Mother Syndrome

To be released in 2005

Companion Workbook

for

Judas's Mother

by Bobbi Sims

We would love to hear your success stories or your pain.
Would you share your challenges
and how they have effected your life?
Please email them to the address below.
Also, for Monthly tips and updates please email us at:
Bobbi@JudasMother.com

Bobbi Sims Presents a Keynote Performance

OVERCOMING THE JUDAS MOTHER SYNDROME

Theater in ancient times consisted of one actor who played all the characters with the aid of different masks. Bobbi Sims has adapted a similar style of presentation.

In period costume, Bobbi plays the role of Mary, the mother of Judas, her friend Amashia, and acts as the commentator making the lessons relevant today.

Mary, the Biblically unmentioned mother of Judas Iscariot, shares her story of taking responsibility for her son's actions and how she was later freed from false responsibility through lessons learned from loving friends, God's teachings, and forgiveness.

A performance to make you cry, to laugh and to think. Mary moves from a position of prestige, to the depths of guilt and shame, and finally to redemption, returning as a teacher of women in her time as well as today.

Whether you are a Biblical history enthusiast, a concerned parent, or simply enjoy a thought-provoking story, this performance will speak to your heart.

PRESENTATION ADAPTED TO THE FOLLOWING AUDIENCES

Women's Groups
Christian Conferences
Rallies
Churches
Conventions
Business Conferences

To book a performance call:
1•800•950•7479
www.JudasMother.com

Judas's Mother

☐ REQUEST FOR INFORMATION   ☐ BOOK ORDER

@ \$17.95 US   plus shipping \$3.00   Total \$20.95 ea
                   Texas residents add   \$1.72

Quantity [   ]   Total [   ]

@ \$25.95 CN   plus shipping \$4.00   Total \$29.95 ea

Quantity [   ]   Total [   ]

PAYMENT

☐ Visa   ☐ Mastercard

Card Number:

[   ] [   ] [   ] [   ]

Ex: [   ]

ADDRESS AS IT APPEARS ON YOUR BILLING ADDRESS:

Name _____

Address _____

City_____ State _____ Zip _____

Day Phone: _____

LET US KNOW IF YOU WISH SHIPPING TO A DIFFERENT ADDRESS:

Name _____

Address _____

City_____ State _____ Zip _____

Fax to: 361•857•7181 or
Mail to: Élan Publishing,
4600 Ocean Drive,
Suite 408,
Corpus Christi, TX 78412